ROMANS

BIBLE STUDY

LIVING OUR
FAITH WITH GRACE
AND TRUTH

✢

KEVIN HARNEY

BASED ON COMMENTARY FROM

DOUGLAS J. MOO

HarperChristian
Resources

Contents

About the Bible Study Series...................................... v

The Letter to the Romans at a Glance vii

1 Faith or Rebellion? (Romans 1:1–7, 8–17, 18–32) 1

2 God's Righteousness (Romans 2:1–16, 17–29; 3:1–8)................. 15

3 Victory Over Sin (Romans 3:9–20, 21–31; 4:1–25) 29

4 A New Perspective on Faith (Romans 5:1–11, 12–14, 15–21) 43

5 From Death to Life (Romans 6:1–10, 11–14, 15–23) 57

6 Faith, Freedom, and Fruitfulness (Romans 7:1–6, 7–12, 13–25) 69

7 No Condemnation (Romans 8:1–13, 18–30, 31–39)................. 83

8 It's All About God (Romans 9:1–13, 19–29; 9:30–10:13)............. 97

9 God's Chosen People (Romans 10:14–11:6; 11:11–24, 25–36)......... 111

10 Sacrificial Living (Romans 12:1–8, 9–21; 13:8–14)................. 125

11 No Stumbling Blocks (Romans 14:1–12, 13–23; 15:1–13) 137

12 Stories of Friendship (Romans 15:14–33; 16:1–16, 17–27) 151

About Kevin Harney and Douglas J. Moo 167

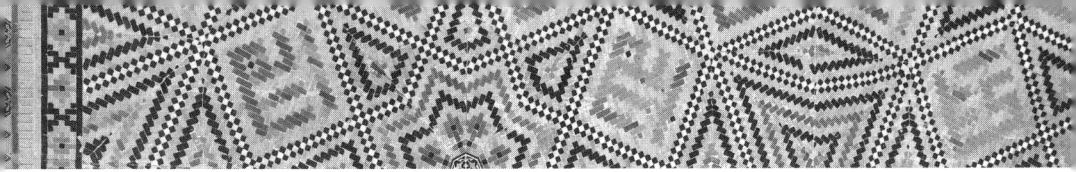

About the

BIBLE STUDY SERIES

Life transformation . . . that is the bottom line. When the Holy Spirit spoke through James and said that followers of Christ are not to "merely listen to the word" but actually "do what it says" (1:22), it was a declaration that academic study of the Bible is not the whole story. God desires for us to read the Bible, seek to understand it in both its *original* context and in *today's* culture, and then allow what we have read to propel us deeper into the will and ways of our Creator.

This is the goal of the series. The vision is for you to first dig into high-level scholarship that plumbs the depths of biblical history, culture, language, and theology. But you won't just stop there! Next, you will connect the ancient words of the Bible to eternal truths and see how they carry throughout to our modern world today. Finally, the goal is for you to see those eternal truths of God come alive in every part of your life.

Each of the studies in the series is based on *The NIV Application Commentary*—one of the most dynamic and well-rounded volumes of commentaries available today. The scholars behind each of these works take readers on a round-trip journey, first back to biblical times and then forward to our times today. Along the way, they dig into deep theological insights that bridge the ancient biblical text to the modern world with theological and interpretive integrity.

Prompts have been provided in each lesson of the series to help guide your experience. Each begins with a brief introduction that identifies a key theme for that session. You will then read the biblical text you will be studying. (**Note that these are selected texts and not every passage in the book of the Bible that you are studying may be covered.**) Try to read every passage slowly, thoughtfully, and prayerfully.

Each biblical passage is followed by an **Original Meaning** section, drawn from *The NIV Application Commentary,* that will help you understand the author's original intent behind the writing and how the original readers would have interpreted that text. This is followed by the **Past to Present** section, which is intended to help you bridge the gap between the ancient and modern and understand how to apply what you just read to your situation today.

You will find **application and reflection questions** in every lesson to help you in this regard. If you are doing this study on your own, use them for reflection, journaling, and digging deeper into your own growth in faith. If you are walking through this study with a few friends or in a small group, use them for group discussion and interaction.

Finally, at the end of each session is a brief **prayer** prompt. This is designed to be a launchpad into a time of personal prayer around the major theme or themes of the session. Use this prayer as a prompt to help you seek God, gain the understanding that he wants you to have, and discover his power at work in your life.

It will be a great adventure . . . so let's begin!

The Letter to the Romans at a Glance

Author: The opening verse of Romans states that the letter was written by "Paul, a servant of Jesus Christ, called to be an apostle" (1:1). More accurately, the letter was composed by Paul, who used a scribe named Tertius to write down what he dictated to him (see 16:22).

Date: Most scholars believe that Paul wrote the letter to the Romans while in Corinth during his third missionary journey (see Acts 20:2–3). This would place the date of writing c. AD 57.

Setting: Paul had never been to Rome, but he was planning on making a journey to Spain (see Romans 15:24), and his hope was to stop in Rome and get the support of Christians there in that endeavor. Paul recognized that as both a faithful Jew and God's "point man" in opening the Gentile mission, he was constantly under suspicion in the church. The Jewish Christians thought he was giving too much of the old tradition away, while the Gentile Christians thought he was still too Jewish. Many false rumors about his teachings and actions were swirling about him (see 3:8), and Paul understood he would need to clear the air if he expected the Romans to support him. Therefore, it is argued, he wrote Romans to clarify just what he believed.

Focus: Romans cries out through history, "Faith is not passive!" There is truth. There is falsehood. Believers can know the difference, turn from darkness, and walk in the light of Jesus. In God's sovereignty, he calls us to himself and offers grace. As living sacrifices, we surrender ourselves to his will and ways. As we walk in the truth, we live with the confidence that nothing can separate us from God's love as revealed and offered through Jesus.

Faith or Rebellion?

Romans 1:1–7, 8–17, 18–32

We make decisions every day that set the trajectory of our lives. Some seem small and insignificant. Others feel epic and important. All are leading us *somewhere*. In the first chapter of Romans, we are given a picture of the choices the human race has taken when it comes to acknowledging God's sovereignty and giving him glory. Sadly, what we find is a series of poor decisions made by humans since the dawn of time. It is a powerful image of the downward spiral we all can travel when we choose rebellion over following God.

You've seen this play out. A child visits a neighbor and admires her new friend's colored markers. So she decides to slip a few into her pocket . . . even though she knows it is wrong. A teenage boy decides to go out partying with his buddies . . . even though his parents have forbidden it. A couple of coworkers decide to use company time, materials, and resources for personal gain . . . even though they know it goes against company policy and their own sense of right and wrong. In each case, a cycle of sin has started. A rebellion has occurred.

Paul declares the best way to break such sinful patterns is through genuine and Spirit-led faith in Christ. Jesus offers power for dramatic and consistent transformation. When we follow him and walk in his ways, everything changes for us. Our life's direction, motives, dreams, and relationships come under the lordship of the Savior. Where sin was in charge, faith now takes over. We begin to make decisions each day to walk in faith rather than stay in the downward cycle of sin. This is the hope we find in the opening chapter of Romans.

Called to Faith in Christ [Romans 1:1-7]

[1] Paul, a servant of Christ Jesus, called to be an apostle and set apart for the gospel of God— [2] the gospel he promised beforehand through his prophets in the Holy Scriptures [3] regarding his Son, who as to his earthly life was a descendant of David, [4] and who through the Spirit of holiness was appointed the Son of God in power by his resurrection from the dead: Jesus Christ our Lord. [5] Through him we received grace and apostleship to call all the Gentiles to the obedience that comes from faith for his name's sake. [6] And you also are among those Gentiles who are called to belong to Jesus Christ.

[7] To all in Rome who are loved by God and called to be his holy people: Grace and peace to you from God our Father and from the Lord Jesus Christ.

Original Meaning

Paul introduces himself to the Roman Christians by identifying his *master*, his *office*, and his *purpose*. While the term *servant* reveals Paul's subservience to his Lord (his master), it was also applied to outstanding figures in Israel's history, such as Moses and David. Paul is "called to be an apostle" (his office), one of those whom Jesus himself had appointed to represent him and to provide the foundation for his church (see Ephesians 2:20). "Set apart for the gospel of God" (his purpose) probably refers to the time when God called him on the Damascus Road.

The gospel is the central, unifying motif of Romans, and Paul signals its importance by referring to it three other times in his introduction (see Romans 1:9, 15–16). Throughout his letter, he is at pains to demonstrate the good news about Jesus is rooted firmly in the soil of the Old Testament. Jesus' resurrection—concluding and validating his messianic work of redemption—gave him power to provide salvation to all who would believe in him.

Paul ends his introduction by elaborating on his apostolic status (see verses 5–6). He has received the grace of being an apostle for two purposes. First, from the time of his conversion, the Lord made clear to him that his primary mission was to bring Gentiles to faith in Jesus. What marks God's people would no longer be deeds done in obedience to the law but an obedience that stems from, accompanies, and displays faith. Second, the Christians in Rome are included among those Gentiles. In this, one of Paul's concerns in his letter is to establish his right to address a group of Christians whom he has never met before.

❖ What does Paul say about the nature of the *gospel* that he preaches?

_____

_____

_____

_____

Past to Present

When it comes to determining how this passage applies to us in the *present*, we first have to look at what it meant to the original readers in the *past*. We will discover that there are timeless truths that can guide us today, much as they did in the time of the Bible.

Even Serving Is a Gift of Grace

In the opening of Paul's letter to the Romans, we find his chosen designation for himself: "a servant of Christ Jesus, called to be an apostle and set apart for the gospel" (verse 1). Paul had not always chosen to identify himself in this way. Rather, his past was one of persecuting the church and celebrating the murder of Christians (see Acts 8:1–3; 26:10). Simply put, he had a dark history. He did not deserve to be called a servant of Jesus or an apostle. Yet this is exactly what *God* called him. He set Paul apart to spread the gospel to the world.

We, like Paul, also have a dark history. We have fallen short of God's standard—and do not deserve to be called a servant of Christ. Yet serving Jesus and his church is *not* based on merit. We don't earn this right. In fact, we *can't* earn it. So it is that when we look into the mirror and ask ourselves if we are worthy to serve with the gifts God has given us, the response back from him is always filled with grace. God doesn't call us because we have made ourselves acceptable. No, his calling on our lives is a gift of grace. The privilege of serving Jesus, his church, and the world is based on *God's* power and not our performance.

❖ What is one way God has gifted and called you to serve him (or other people in his name)? How has this calling revealed God's goodness to you and others?

_____

_____

_____

_____

❖ What is one way that God has used you to serve him or the people in your life? What did this process of serving teach you about grace?

_____

_____

_____

_____

The Gospel Is for Everyone
Paul states that the believers in Rome "are among those Gentiles who are called to belong to Jesus Christ" (verse 6). The earliest believers were

those of Jewish heritage who realized Jesus was their long-awaited Messiah. They assumed, at first, that Jesus was just for them and not for the non-Jewish people of the world. This would have been understandable, given the Gentiles (non-Jews) had their own religions and a whole pantheon of gods. Why would they *want* to follow Jesus?

What these early believers learned is that the mission of Jesus is to bring his love, grace, truth, and good news to the entire world. As followers of Jesus, they were called to shine the light of his salvation everywhere that God took them (see Matthew 5:14–16). The promises of God that we read about in the Bible are not just for a select group of individuals—they pertain to each and every one of us. God has extended his grace to us and allowed us to partake in the salvation that Jesus purchased through his death on the cross. The gospel is for *everyone*.

❖ Who shared the gospel with you? How did they articulate it in a way that made sense and helped you embrace Jesus by faith?

❖ Who in your life needs to hear the good news about Jesus? How are you seeking to communicate this message of hope to that person?

Encouraged by Faith [Romans 1:8–17]

[8] First, I thank my God through Jesus Christ for all of you, because your faith is being reported all over the world. [9] God, whom I serve in my spirit

in preaching the gospel of his Son, is my witness how constantly I remember you [10] in my prayers at all times; and I pray that now at last by God's will the way may be opened for me to come to you.

[11] I long to see you so that I may impart to you some spiritual gift to make you strong— [12] that is, that you and I may be mutually encouraged by each other's faith. [13] I do not want you to be unaware, brothers and sisters, that I planned many times to come to you (but have been prevented from doing so until now) in order that I might have a harvest among you, just as I have had among the other Gentiles.

[14] I am obligated both to Greeks and non-Greeks, both to the wise and the foolish. [15] That is why I am so eager to preach the gospel also to you who are in Rome.

[16] For I am not ashamed of the gospel, because it is the power of God that brings salvation to everyone who believes: first to the Jew, then to the Gentile. [17] For in the gospel the righteousness of God is revealed—a righteousness that is by faith from first to last, just as it is written: "The righteous will live by faith."

Original Meaning

Paul expresses his thanksgiving to God "through Jesus Christ," for it is Jesus who has created the access that enables him to approach God in thanksgiving. The cause of Paul's thankfulness is the reputation the Roman Christians have gained for their faith and acts of service. Paul reveals not only that he knows this about them but also that he continually prays for them and desires to visit them to impart "some spiritual gift" (verse 11). Paul may have in mind an insight or ability given by the Spirit that he wants to share with them to strengthen their faith.

Paul's zeal for preaching the gospel is so great that he feels "obligated" to share it "both to Greeks and non-Greeks" (verse 14). This is why he is so eager and motivated to make the journey to Rome to be with them. Few of us will ever have such clear direction about a call to ministry or about the direction that our ministry should take. However, Paul's words reveal that the imperative to evangelize is an *obligation* that all believers in Christ share.

Paul's eagerness comes from knowing the gospel he preaches is God's divinely appointed means for bringing salvation to the world. The terms *salvation (sōtēria)* and *save (sōzō)* will prove to be important in Romans. Paul uses them to describe not only a person's conversion but also the final deliverance from sin and evil that will be completed at one's death or the end of all things. Paul, announcing what will become a key theme in this letter, insists the salvation available in the gospel is for "everyone who believes" (verse 16).

❖ What was the role and place of the gospel in Paul's life? What should it be in the life of every follower of Jesus?

_____

_____

_____

_____

Past to Present

A Call to Love

When Jesus was asked about the most significant and important commandment, his response was clear and piercing: to love God and to love other people (see Matthew 22:37–40). When you read the opening words of Romans, you can feel the love of God pouring through Paul for the believers in the community and for those who did not yet know Jesus. He once had been a persecutor of the church, but now he was one who loved all of God's people.

The call to share God's love extends to believers today. So . . . how is *your* love level today? Can you say that you are deeply in love with Jesus?

Do you delight in your fellow brothers and sisters in Christ and celebrate their spiritual growth? Does your heart break for those who are still wandering like sheep far from the Good Shepherd? After all, Paul's call is also your call: to love God, love his people, and love the lost.

❖ Who is a person you know who is growing in faith? How can you encourage and cheer that person on in his or her faith journey?

❖ What are some of the evangelistic ministries in your church? How might you engage more in these efforts to shine the light of Jesus in your community?

A Life of Faith

None of us are capable of making ourselves worthy of salvation. Not even the best among us. The gospel is "good news" because it announces that God accepts us anyway. All we must do is receive God's offer in faith. However, at the same time, true faith is always accompanied by *obedience*. This balance of receiving God's grace and walking in surrender to his will is the pathway that each follower of Jesus must travel.

Paul writes that "in the gospel the righteousness of God is revealed" (verse 17). When we receive salvation through the gospel and come to faith in Christ, we start to understand God's righteousness and the kind of life he desires us to lead. We won't get this right every time. Following Jesus is an adventure of joy-filled victory and tearful stumbling. However, what we can know for certain is that Jesus is transforming us. His Holy Spirit now resides in us and empowers us to walk in the ways that God has established for us.

❖ How would you describe the balance you see in your life between receiving God's grace and walking in surrender to his will?

_____

_____

_____

_____

_____

❖ What is an area of your life that you know God is in the process of transforming? What evidence can you see of how far God has taken you in this journey?

_____

_____

_____

_____

The Deadly Cycle of Sin [Romans 1:18–32]

[18] The wrath of God is being revealed from heaven against all the godlessness and wickedness of people, who suppress the truth by their wickedness, [19] since what may be known about God is plain to them, because God has made it plain to them. [20] For since the creation of the world God's invisible qualities—his eternal power and divine nature—have been clearly seen, being understood from what has been made, so that people are without excuse.

[21] For although they knew God, they neither glorified him as God nor gave thanks to him, but their thinking became futile and their foolish hearts were darkened. [22] Although they claimed to be wise, they became fools [23] and exchanged the glory of the immortal God for images made to look like a mortal human being and birds and animals and reptiles.

[24] Therefore God gave them over in the sinful desires of their hearts to sexual impurity for the degrading of their bodies with one another. [25] They exchanged the truth about God for a lie, and worshiped and served created things rather than the Creator—who is forever praised. Amen.

[26] Because of this, God gave them over to shameful lusts. Even their women exchanged natural sexual relations for unnatural ones. [27] In the same way the men also abandoned natural relations with women and were inflamed with lust for one another. Men committed shameful acts with other men, and received in themselves the due penalty for their error.

[28] Furthermore, just as they did not think it worthwhile to retain the knowledge of God, so God gave them over to a depraved mind, so that they do what ought not to be done. [29] They have become filled with every kind of wickedness, evil, greed and depravity. They are full of envy, murder, strife, deceit and malice. They are gossips, [30] slanderers, God-haters, insolent, arrogant and boastful; they invent ways of doing evil; they disobey their parents; [31] they have no understanding, no fidelity, no love, no mercy. [32] Although they know God's righteous decree that those who do such things deserve death, they not only continue to do these very things but also approve of those who practice them.

Original Meaning

Paul's abrupt shift in topic comes as a surprise. We would expect him to expound on the truths that he has just proclaimed about the gospel. Instead, he launches into a discussion about "the wrath of God" against sinful humanity (verse 18). Evidently, Paul's purpose in doing this is to explain why the revelation of God's righteousness in the gospel is necessary. Only by fully understanding the *bad news* can we then fully appreciate the *good news*.

The reaction of God to sin that Paul depicts is not that of an "emotional" person but a necessary response of a holy God to spiritual rebellion. The Old Testament prophets regularly spoke of God's wrath on people, both in the course of history and at the end of history. Paul is thus likely referring broadly to the sentence of condemnation all people fall under—a sentence the Lord sometimes inflicts in the events of history but will carry out with finality at the end of time. We don't like to think of God's judgment, but it is essential that we fully understand the cost of sin and the consequences of spiritual rebellion against God.

God's wrath falls on those who "suppress the truth" (verse 18). A person can only suppress something of which he or she has knowledge. Humans *do* have knowledge about God, for he has made this knowledge "plain to them" (verse 19) through the created world around them. Moreover, these qualities "have been clearly seen" (verse 20). God has made himself known—even though people have not wanted to admit it!

Three times Paul in this passage repeats a heartbreaking sequence: they "exchanged" (verses 23, 25, 26) and "God gave them over" (verses 24, 26, 28). Humans set up their own gods or chose to engage in sin instead of accepting the truth that God revealed. The Lord reacted to this rebellion by handing them over to the choices they made. The language gives the picture of God stepping back and allowing people to live with the consequences of the sinful decisions they have made.

❖ How does Paul describe wickedness in this passage? How does he describe God's wrath?

_____

_____

_____

_____

_____

Past to Present

Break the Cycle

If you have walked with those who are struggling with an addiction, you know they often have to hit rock bottom before they look up for help. This is true for all of us when battling sin. Until we come to the point where we throw it down, repent, and call out for God's help, we remain in its clutches—and even approve of others who do the same.

This refusal to "look up" leads to the downward spiritual cycle of sin that Paul describes in this passage. We exchange worship of God for worship of our idols. We exchange the truth God provides with the lies of the enemy. We exchange the life God wants us to lead with the life the world compels us to live. The only way out of this destructive cycle is to refuse to make the "exchange" in the first place—to worship only *God*, accept *his* truth, and faithfully obey *his* commands.

❖ How do you respond to Paul's description of humanity's rebellion against God? How do you see your actions in what Paul describes?

_____

_____

_____

_____

_____

❖ What are some examples of how the culture approves of sinful behaviors that God clearly condemns? Why would this kind of approval (and even celebration) evoke God's righteous anger?

_____

_____

_____

_____

_____

What Nature Reveals

Paul's assertion is not only that God has left clear evidence of himself in the world he made but also that people have perceived this evidence—that "God has made it plain to them" (verse 19). What Paul is stating is that *creation* points to a *Creator*. As the psalmist declared, "The heavens declare the glory of God; the skies proclaim the work of his hands" (Psalm 19:1). If we want evidence that God exists, we need only look at the intricacies of our planet and the universe. All of God's works in the natural world reveal his presence.

This reality of "natural revelation" and its availability to everyone addresses one of the most often-asked questions about God's justice: *What about those who have never heard?* Most of us have wondered how God, in his love and justice, will deal with those who have never had the chance to hear the message of salvation. The question has no easy answer, but what we can assert is that all people, in some way, *have* heard. God has revealed certain truths about himself in the world, and all people have access to that truth.

Of course, this doesn't mean that sharing the gospel is unimportant. Paul certainly didn't adopt that view—in spite of the comments he made about natural revelation. Sharing the message of God's grace and the hope found in Jesus remains the call of *every* believer.

❖ What are some of the ways God reveals himself through creation and the natural world? How do you see and encounter God in his intricate and beautiful world?

❖ Creation does not fully reveal the message of Jesus, but it can help people identify and embrace a divine Creator. What methods have you found effective when it comes to helping people see that God does exist and wants to have a relationship with us?

_____

_____

_____

_____

_____

_____

Closing Prayer: *Heavenly Father, reveal your presence and power to me through all you have made. Help me to be a force in this world who helps people break the cycle of sin and accept you as their Lord and Savior. I surrender my life to following you by faith and ask that you will help me turn from the enticement of sin in this world. In the powerful name of Jesus. Amen.*

2

God's Righteousness

Romans 2:1-16, 17-29; 3:1-8

Couples go through many stages in a relationship, starting with attraction. This is when the relationship is brand-new and everything the other person says and does seems so witty, and funny, and thoughtful. It's as if the couple is looking at each other through rose-colored glasses. There may be major red flags, but everything appears rosy.

We all view life through our own set of filters. The problem is—much like a couple in the early stages of their relationship—our vision can get clouded. Our outlook can get out of sync with how God sees things. This is why we need to learn how to view things through the eyes of our Creator. It is only when we are willing to remove the rose-colored glasses that we are able to identify the faults and flaws in our lives. When we do this, we find that God is patient and kind to forgive our sins and restore us into a right relationship with him.

In this section of Romans, Paul explores this theme of what it means to look at things through a divine perspective. He shows us how God is righteous even when we are not. How God is faithful even when we plunge into unfaithfulness and judge others for the sins that we ourselves are guilty of committing. And how God is concerned more on the condition of our hearts than on our external behavior. We gravitate toward following rules and regulations, but God delights when we freely walk in his ways and follow him with a willing heart.

Do Not Judge Others [Romans 2:1–16]

[1] You, therefore, have no excuse, you who pass judgment on someone else, for at whatever point you judge another, you are condemning yourself, because you who pass judgment do the same things. [2] Now we know that God's judgment against those who do such things is based on truth. [3] So when you, a mere human being, pass judgment on them and yet do the same things, do you think you will escape God's judgment? [4] Or do you show contempt for the riches of his kindness, forbearance and patience, not realizing that God's kindness is intended to lead you to repentance?

[5] But because of your stubbornness and your unrepentant heart, you are storing up wrath against yourself for the day of God's wrath, when his righteous judgment will be revealed. [6] God "will repay each person according to what they have done." [7] To those who by persistence in doing good seek glory, honor and immortality, he will give eternal life. [8] But for those who are self-seeking and who reject the truth and follow evil, there will be wrath and anger. [9] There will be trouble and distress for every human being who does evil: first for the Jew, then for the Gentile; [10] but glory, honor and peace for everyone who does good: first for the Jew, then for the Gentile. [11] For God does not show favoritism.

[12] All who sin apart from the law will also perish apart from the law, and all who sin under the law will be judged by the law. [13] For it is not those who hear the law who are righteous in God's sight, but it is those who obey the law who will be declared righteous. [14] (Indeed, when Gentiles, who do not have the law, do by nature things required by the law, they are a law for themselves, even though they do not have the law. [15] They show that the requirements of the law are written on their hearts, their consciences also bearing witness, and their thoughts sometimes accusing them and at other times even defending them.) [16] This will take place on the day when God judges people's secrets through Jesus Christ, as my gospel declares.

Original Meaning

Paul changes his language in this passage to address a specific group of people, saying, "*You*, therefore, have no excuse." This group, Paul will later reveal, is the Jews, who "pass judgment on someone else"—the Gentiles (verse 1). Paul says that God's judgment against them is "based on truth." It is just, impartial, and founded on facts. Furthermore, their attempts to rely on "the riches of [God's] kindness, forbearance and patience" shown to them in the past will not work when it comes to avoiding this judgment. Paul's words connote God's grace and willingness to forgive, but they must be willing to repent and turn from sin.

It's easy to judge the Jews for their judgment, but their assumption of superiority over Gentiles was not a matter of ego or personal boasting. Out of all the nations of the earth, God had chosen Israel as his people. The Jews may have reasoned, as God's chosen people, that they were immune from judgment. It is this assumption that Paul attacks. God's kindness was intended to lead them to repentance. Instead, it appears they were regarding it as a carte blanche to sin with impunity. As a result, Paul concludes, the Jews are "storing up wrath" against themselves (verse 5)—a wrath that will be inflicted on the day of God's coming righteous judgment. This represents a sober warning for Paul's audience and for us today.

In effect, Paul argues, there is a level playing field when it comes to God's verdict: God "will repay each person according to what they have done" (verse 6). Key to Paul's argument is the phrase "each person"—meaning it includes both Jews and Gentiles. Paul makes a similar point in verse 11 by insisting that God "does not show favoritism." The word for *favoritism* was evidently coined by Christians to translate a Hebrew expression that conveys the sense of partiality: treating someone on the basis of outward appearance. God does not do this.

Paul states it is not those who "hear the law" but those who "obey the law" who are declared righteous (verse 13). The apostle here is simply asserting the standard of God's assessment (see also 2:10). No person—other than Jesus—has actually ever been able to meet the standard of obeying the law that is required for right standing with God.

❖ How would you summarize Paul's teaching about judging others?

_____

_____

_____

_____

Past to Present

Consider what this passage meant to the original readers and how it applies to us today.

God Takes Sin Seriously

It is easy to judge the people around us, but Jesus warns us not to spend our time seeking to extract a sliver from the eye of another person when we have a beam in our own (see Matthew 7:3). In a similar manner, Paul teaches that when we pass judgment on others, we are also pointing a finger at ourselves because we are also guilty of sin. So, rather than engaging in building a case against our neighbor, colleague, spouse, or a stranger, we are better off turning our attention to God's kindness and repenting of our sins.

Repentance on our part is critical. Each of us—like the Jews whom Paul was addressing in this passage—can show contempt for God's kindness toward us. We can grow cavalier toward our sin because we think God will simply overlook it out of his love for us in Christ. But sin is a serious matter to the Lord! Although the Bible states that believers are eternally secure in Christ, it is also clear that a lack of concern about our sin is incompatible with true faith. Thus, Paul's warning about presuming on God's grace carries a stark warning for us.

❖ Why is it often easier to focus on the sins of *others* and miss seeing your *own* failings? Why is this dangerous for your spiritual health?

_____

_____

_____

_____

_____

❖ What are some ways that you can keep your heart tuned into the weight, cost, and seriousness of sin? Why is it essential for you to never forget God's hatred of sin?

_____

_____

_____

_____

_____

God Judges Our Hearts

Paul discusses a question in this passage that we all wonder about at times: *Do we have the power to please God and obey his will?* Paul asserts the power to obey God is universally available to all who receive it by faith. This is encouraging! Yet he also states this reality will include God judging the secrets of our hearts through Jesus. This is challenging!

Appearing righteous on the *outside* is one thing, but being righteous on the *inside*—in every thought—seems impossible. The good news is that even though God reaches into our deepest sin and judges us, he does so not to bring shame on us but to heal us and set us free for the relationship he offers. We are not in this alone! Our response, then, should be to welcome God's judgment. Once we get a glimpse of what it is like to be in full fellowship with him, we won't want any barriers or secrets to keep us from him again. We will desire to see the fruit of holiness and righteousness in our lives—and want to obey him.

❖ When is a time that God challenged you on your thoughts? How did that action on his part result in greater obedience to him?

_____

_____

_____

_____

❖ Paul says it is those who *obey* the law who will be declared righteous. What is an instruction you've *heard* God say to you but have yet to put into *practice*? What steps will you take today to actually put that instruction into practice?

_____

_____

_____

_____

True Jewishness [Romans 2:17–29]

[17] Now you, if you call yourself a Jew; if you rely on the law and boast in God; [18] if you know his will and approve of what is superior because you are instructed by the law; [19] if you are convinced that you are a guide for the blind, a light for those who are in the dark, [20] an instructor of the foolish, a teacher of little children, because you have in the law the embodiment of knowledge and truth— [21] you, then, who teach others, do you not teach yourself? You who preach against stealing, do you steal? [22] You who say that people should not commit adultery, do you commit adultery? You who abhor idols, do you rob temples? [23] You who boast in the law, do you dishonor God by breaking the law? [24] As it is written: "God's name is blasphemed among the Gentiles because of you."

[25] Circumcision has value if you observe the law, but if you break the law, you have become as though you had not been circumcised. [26] So then, if those who are not circumcised keep the law's requirements, will they

not be regarded as though they were circumcised? [27] The one who is not circumcised physically and yet obeys the law will condemn you who, even though you have the written code and circumcision, are a lawbreaker.

[28] A person is not a Jew who is one only outwardly, nor is circumcision merely outward and physical. [29] No, a person is a Jew who is one inwardly; and circumcision is circumcision of the heart, by the Spirit, not by the written code. Such a person's praise is not from other people, but from God.

Original Meaning

Paul now touches on two of the most distinguishing marks of being Jewish: (1) possession of the law and (2) the covenant sign of circumcision. He previously stated it is *doing* God's will—not *knowing* it or *teaching* it—that matters when it comes to God's judgment. This is where the Jews have fallen short. They "boast" about their relationship with God and the fact they have been "instructed by the law" (verses 17–18), but they do not live up to these boasts.

Paul's charge is that the Jews know the law and teach others about it but do not teach themselves. He cites examples of their hypocrisy: they steal, commit adultery, "rob temples" (perhaps a statement against relaxing the Old Testament restrictions related to using precious metals melted down from pagan idols), and generally dishonor God by breaking his law (see verses 21–23). As a result of these transgressions, "God's name is blasphemed among the Gentiles" (verse 24).

When it comes to circumcision, Paul does not deny it has value. However, this value is contingent on obedience: Only those who "observe the law" profit from it (verse 25). The problem is that the Jews' obedience to the law never reaches the high mark required to escape God's wrath—and this failure annuls the value of circumcision. Paul concludes that true "Jewishness" is not determined by physical birth, or devotion to the law, or participating in acts like circumcision. To be a real Jew is an inward matter. It is marked by a "circumcision of the heart" that comes through the work of the Holy Spirit.

❖ What spiritual wake-up call was Paul giving to the Jews in this passage? What was he pointing out about the security they felt they had merely because they were Jews?

_____

_____

_____

_____

Past to Present

A Wake-Up Call

Have you ever had a friend give you a wake-up call? Perhaps you were headed in a certain direction and your friend stepped in to say that you were heading off course. Or maybe you were making a series of bad decisions and your friend warned you of the consequences. Or it could be that you were holding on to a grudge and your friend advised you to let go of your grievance.

This is what the Holy Spirit is doing through Paul when it comes to addressing the Jews. The Lord is speaking the truth to his people that they needed to hear. Now, before we dismiss Paul's words as being *just* for the Jews of his day, we need to acknowledge we are guilty of many of the same things that he points out in this passage. We, too, suffer from pride at times—from "bragging" about our relationship with Christ without living up to our boasts.

This is why the piercing list that Paul provides in verses 17–20 can be helpful to us. Paul is offering up a number of traits that might indicate we have fallen into pride when it comes to our spirituality. This is not to say we will *never* drift into this territory. Rather, like a trusted friend who gives us a wake-up call, Paul is helping us to see if the general trajectory of our lives is headed off track and pride is leading us to a general condition of spiritual blindness. If so, we can make course corrections to get ourselves back in line with God's will.

❖ When is a time that God lovingly and boldly gave you a wake-up call to let you know that you were heading into a place that you spiritually should not go?

_____

_____

_____

_____

_____

❖ What are some traits Paul lists in verses 17–20 that might be present in your life? What do you need to do to rid yourself of those traits?

_____

_____

_____

_____

Circumcision of the Heart

Circumcision was first instituted by God as a sign of his covenant with Abraham (see Genesis 17:9–13) and routinely practiced in Israel from that time forward. However, with the rise in Hellenistic ways of thinking around the time of the Maccabean Revolt (166–160 BC), and with more and more Jews mingling with Gentiles, pious Jews naturally began to afford greater importance to the rite of circumcision as way of keeping themselves separate from the world.

Paul's claim, however, is that the *physical* act of circumcision has no meaning if it is not accompanied by a *spiritual* act. We do not become the people of God because of our physical birth, or any cuts we make on our skin, or by our devotion to a particular book. Rather, we become God's people through an inward "circumcision" of the heart—a circumcision that comes by the work of the Holy Spirit in our lives. Only those who, through faith in Christ, have received the Spirit of God and submitted to him will truly make up God's people.

❖ What are some of the ways that Christians today try to keep themselves separate from the world? What are some of these practices that you employ in your life?

_____

_____

_____

_____

❖ What are some ways you reveal to God that you want to be included among his people? What does it look like in your life to truly submit to the work of the Holy Spirit?

_____

_____

_____

_____

God's Enduring Faithfulness [Romans 3:1–8]

[1] What advantage, then, is there in being a Jew, or what value is there in circumcision? [2] Much in every way! First of all, the Jews have been entrusted with the very words of God.

[3] What if some were unfaithful? Will their unfaithfulness nullify God's faithfulness? [4] Not at all! Let God be true, and every human being a liar. As it is written:

"So that you may be proved right when you speak
and prevail when you judge."

[5] But if our unrighteousness brings out God's righteousness more clearly, what shall we say? That God is unjust in bringing his wrath on us? (I am using a human argument.) [6] Certainly not! If that were so, how could God judge the world? [7] Someone might argue, "If my falsehood enhances God's truthfulness and so increases his glory, why am I still condemned as a sinner?" [8] Why not say—as some slanderously claim that we say—"Let us do evil that good may result"? Their condemnation is just!

Original Meaning

Paul has just spent a chapter arguing that Jews and Gentiles stand in the same position before God. Given this, his opening question, "What advantage, then, is there in being a Jew?" (verse 1), should naturally lead to a response of "none." But instead, Paul answers his own question by stating, "Much in every way!" (verse 2). He does not want his previous argument to leave the impression in his readers' minds that *all* the Jews' privileges have been revoked.

After all, Paul states, the unfaithfulness on the part of the Jewish people can never nullify God's faithfulness toward them. However, this does not mean the Jews are immune from God's righteous judgment as a *result* of their unfaithfulness. Some were evidently claiming that a person's falsehood enhances God's truthfulness and thus brings him glory. Yet such an idea would mean that sin is *justified* as long as it eventually brings about a greater good. In Paul's mind, it was right and just for those who thought this way—and who actually engaged in practicing evil so "good may result" (verse 8)—to be condemned.

Just imagine what would happen if followers of God decided to sin as much as they wanted because of a misguided belief that human rebellion unleashes heavenly grace. What would the world look like? How would the church function? What would our lives become? We can only speculate at the amount of depravity and destruction that would be unleashed. This is the mindset Paul is countering here. He is correcting a perverted theology that took grace lightly, mocked the cost of sin, and took advantage of the sacrifice of Jesus.

❖ What does Paul say is the advantage in being a Jew? What point does he then make by stating that some of the Jews were unfaithful to God (see verses 1–4)?

_____

_____

_____

_____

_____

_____

Past to Present

God's Enduring Faithfulness

Faithfulness has fallen on hard times lately. There was a day when people followed one sports team for a lifetime. There was a time when the phrase "until death do us part" meant a couple stayed in the relationship through the ups and downs of life. There was a generation that joined a church and stayed there even if the pastor's message convicted them at times.

These statements are not meant to be critical—they are just reminders that the world has changed. People move more often and shift allegiances with greater ease. Faithfulness is not held up as a desirable virtue in the way it was in the past. However, in spite of our own human tendencies, we can be certain that God always remains faithful. He is the same "yesterday and today and forever" (Hebrews 13:8), which means that he is faithful even when we are not.

❖ What are some ways that God has been faithful to you in your life? How have you seen his relentless faithfulness even when your devotion to him wavered?

_____

_____

_____

_____

❖ How should the faithfulness of God impact the way you are faithful in areas such as your marriage, your friendships, and your interactions with other believers in Christ?

_____

_____

_____

_____

Creative Justification of Sin

Our human ability to justify sin is shocking. We can lie and tell ourselves that we are protecting others who can't handle the truth—that our deception is really an act of love! We can steal time and materials from our employer and justify the theft by saying we are not paid enough for our hard work. We can engage in an emotional or physical affair and blame our spouse for not being romantic enough or understanding our needs. The list of justifications for sin grows longer and longer as we creatively convince ourselves that, in our case, it is okay.

It appears that some of the people in Paul's day were taking justification of sin to new levels. They were actually claiming a person's deceit could enhance God's truthfulness and bring him glory. These individuals were not just deceptively covering their tracks but boldly claiming their sin served a good purpose. We may not approach the justification of our sin in the same way, but we need to recognize God views all sin as *sin*. While some sins carry greater earthly consequences, all sins are equal to God—and thus all have eternal consequences.

❖ What are some examples you have seen of how people try to justify their bad behaviors today? Why do you think it is so easy to delude ourselves in this way?

_____

_____

_____

_____

_____

❖ How do you recognize when you are drifting into justifying a sinful behavior? What steps do you take to correct this situation when you see it is happening?

_____

_____

_____

_____

Closing Prayer: *Thank you, Lord, for your never-ending righteousness that shines like a light in this world. I rejoice in your faithfulness toward me even when my sin and rebellion reveal my lack of faith in you. Capture my heart and teach me to willingly surrender to all you have planned for me. I do not want to spend my life struggling to follow rules and regulations. What I long for is a life that reflects your righteousness and faithfulness and that leads to joyful surrender to your lordship each and every day! In the power of Jesus, I pray. Amen.*

3

Victory Over Sin

Romans 3:9-20, 21-31; 4:1-25

Climbing to the summit of Mount Everest is the pinnacle of mountaineering. It is no easy feat! It requires a massive amount of physical training, world-class equipment, and help from those who know the mountain. Victory comes at a high cost. Even those who give all they have to attain the goal have a slim chance of making it.

In the spiritual world, finding victory over sin can seem like a climb to the top of Everest. How can mere humans accomplish the feat? We may assume the answer comes through massive amounts of "training" on our part—work harder, do better, produce more. So much of life works this way. We don't win at sports without practice. Academic advancement demands diligence. Many of our relationships are based on a quid pro quo view of life. So why wouldn't our pathway to cleansing from sin be based on how we perform, behave, and produce?

It is this kind of thinking that leads many people to approach God with fear and efforts to appease. However, the apostle Paul, with logic and compassion, presents a radical and fresh perspective. Victory over sin, cleansing of past wrongs, and true righteousness are not earned or based on *personal* merit but are found in the grace of *Jesus*, the price he paid, and his finished work on the cross. So, while victory over sin does come at a high cost, Jesus has already paid the price. Our role is simply to accept the gift of grace that God offers.

The Universal Impact of Sin [Romans 3:9–20]

[9] What shall we conclude then? Do we have any advantage? Not at all! For we have already made the charge that Jews and Gentiles alike are all under the power of sin. [10] As it is written:

> "There is no one righteous, not even one;
>> [11] there is no one who understands;
>> there is no one who seeks God.
> [12] All have turned away,
>> they have together become worthless;
> there is no one who does good,
>> not even one."
> [13] "Their throats are open graves;
>> their tongues practice deceit."
> "The poison of vipers is on their lips."
>> [14] "Their mouths are full of cursing and bitterness."
> [15] "Their feet are swift to shed blood;
>> [16] ruin and misery mark their ways,
> [17] and the way of peace they do not know."
>> [18] "There is no fear of God before their eyes."

[19] Now we know that whatever the law says, it says to those who are under the law, so that every mouth may be silenced and the whole world held accountable to God. [20] Therefore no one will be declared righteous in God's sight by the works of the law; rather, through the law we become conscious of our sin.

Original Meaning

Paul has been addressing in Romans 3 whether there are any differences between Jews and Gentiles now that Jesus has come. He first asserted that Jews do have certain privileges (verses 1–2) but that this doesn't exempt them (or anyone else) from God's judgment (verses 3–8). Rather, "Jews and Gentiles alike are all under the power of sin" (verse 9). The phrasing here is important. People do not just *commit* sin but are actually under the *power* of sin.

Paul supports this claim by drawing on a set of quotations from the books of Psalms, Ecclesiastes, and Isaiah. His first set of quotations stresses the *universality of sin*—emphasizing that "no one [is] righteous" and "there is no one who does good" (verses 10–12). His second set focuses on *sins of speech*. "Graves," "poison," and "cursing and bitterness" (verses 13–14) all depict the power of sin that is alive in our words. Paul's third set covers *sins of violence*. Our swiftness to "shed blood," cause "ruin and misery," and reject "the way of peace" (verses 15–17) are often a result of our rebellious actions. In the end, what we discover is that human beings have a basic lack of the "fear of God" (verse 18).

Paul concludes the Jews are therefore condemned "under the law" (verse 19). However, he also finds it legitimate to extend this verdict to *all* people. This only makes sense, for, if God's chosen people are to be held accountable for their sinful attitudes, words, and actions, the same must be true of the people groups who do not know his story and law. In the end, what we find is that the law cannot *save* us but can make us *conscious* of our sin. This is because the law sets forth a record of God's will. In this way, it is like a mirror that reveals just how short we are falling in meeting God's high mark of holiness required for salvation!

❖ What are some of the specific sinful acts and attitudes that Paul identifies in verses 10–19? How do these verses make the point that *everyone* is guilty of sin?

Past to Present

Consider what this passage meant to the original readers and how it applies to us today.

Addicted to Sin

Addictions are plentiful in our world. People can be addicted to all kinds of things—drugs, alcohol, nicotine, food, gambling, shopping, and even social media. Almost everyone has felt the lure of addiction.

Why is addiction so prevalent? According to Paul, the reason is because we are "under the power of sin" (verse 9). We are imprisoned by it and unable to free ourselves from it. This is why God did not send us a coach, politician, or cheerleader. He sent a *liberator* who has the power to set us free from our sins. Jesus came to teach, encourage, and lead us, but his ultimate reason for coming was to save us. He is the chain breaker, sin crusher, and the victor over the grave and death.

❖ As you look around at the world, your culture, your circle of friends and relationships, and your own life, what are some signs that sin is addictive and prevalent?

❖ What is one specific area of your life in which you have experienced the liberating power of Jesus over sin? How did this liberation come about for you?

Fear of the Lord

Paul quotes from the Old Testament in verses 10–17 to make several important points about sin. First, as just noted, all human beings fall under the power of sin—it is universal. Second, we can see that sin is alive and well today by examining our speech. We lie, we speak ill of others, and we fill our mouths with cursing and bitterness. Third, our sin causes us to inflict harm on others—shedding blood, causing ruin and misery, and rejecting the way of peace.

The final quotation Paul cites in verse 18, from Psalm 36:1, sums up the problem: "There is no fear of God." For unbelievers, this means there is no fear of the judgment that is coming as a result of their refusal to accept Christ's sacrifice for their sins. For believers, this means there is a lack of reverence and awe for God. When we truly fear the Lord, we understand it is only through his mercy that we have a way to be saved from sin. God owes us nothing . . . and we owe him everything. This awe of the Lord should influence our decisions and compel us to pursue godliness—knowing it is how we demonstrate our respect to him.

❖ What immediately comes to mind when you hear the phrase "the fear of the Lord"?

❖ Why is it so critical for you, as a follower of Christ, to fear the Lord? What are some practical ways you are demonstrating that you truly fear the Lord?

Justified by Faith [Romans 3:21–31]

²¹ But now apart from the law the righteousness of God has been made known, to which the Law and the Prophets testify. ²² This righteousness is given through faith in Jesus Christ to all who believe. There is no difference between Jew and Gentile, ²³ for all have sinned and fall short of the glory of God, ²⁴ and all are justified freely by his grace through the redemption that came by Christ Jesus. ²⁵ God presented Christ as a sacrifice of atonement, through the shedding of his blood—to be received by faith. He did this to demonstrate his righteousness, because in his forbearance he had left the sins committed beforehand unpunished— ²⁶ he did it to demonstrate his righteousness at the present time, so as to be just and the one who justifies those who have faith in Jesus.

²⁷ Where, then, is boasting? It is excluded. Because of what law? The law that requires works? No, because of the law that requires faith. ²⁸ For we maintain that a person is justified by faith apart from the works of the law. ²⁹ Or is God the God of Jews only? Is he not the God of Gentiles too? Yes, of Gentiles too, ³⁰ since there is only one God, who will justify the circumcised by faith and the uncircumcised through that same faith. ³¹ Do we, then, nullify the law by this faith? Not at all! Rather, we uphold the law.

Original Meaning

Paul has been painting a depressing picture of the human condition. We are aware of God's mark for holiness as specified under the law, but that knowledge cannot save us—in fact, it can only point out how much we are failing. Fortunately, there *is* a "righteousness of God" available "apart from the law" that comes to "all who believe" (verses 21–22).

There is no difference between Jew and Gentile when it comes to who falls under the power of sin. Rather, "*all* have sinned and fall short of the glory of God" (verse 23, emphasis added). The only way we can be made righteous before God is to be "justified freely by his grace through the redemption that [comes] by Christ Jesus" (verse 24). Paul's use of the word "grace" (*charis*) emphasizes that God does this act of justification freely and without compulsion. He is not pressured or manipulated into extending his love. The term "redemption" (*apolytrosis*) has the basic sense of "to liberate by paying a price." God has liberated us through the price that Jesus paid for our sins on the cross (see verse 25).

Consequently, Paul summarizes, God is both just and the one who justifies. He can accept sinners who put their faith in Jesus and deem them righteous without violating his own just character because Christ fully satisfied his demand that all who commit sin must die. By faith in Christ, all are joined to him—both Jews and Gentiles alike (see verses 29–30). Jesus becomes our representative and his death is accredited to us. God demands holiness, as revealed in the law, but that holiness is attained only through the atoning work of Christ.

❖ What does Paul say is the condition of all humans outside of God's grace? What has Jesus done to make our salvation possible?

_____

_____

_____

_____

Past to Present

The Turning Point

When individuals who have been engaging in a pattern of destructive behaviors finally come to the end of themselves and hit rock bottom, they often look up and take strides to turn the page of their lives. They realize the cost of their foolish choices, cry out to God (sometimes referred to as their "higher power"), and begin a new chapter of life. This process allows them to see themselves for who they really are and gain a new perspective of who they can become.

Paul invites us to do the same when it comes to our relationship with God. When we recognize the hold sin has on us, it should bring us to a rock-bottom realization that we have no hope of freeing ourselves from its grasp. "All have sinned" (verse 23), and thus all are in need of a Savior. God has liberated us through the price Jesus paid on the cross. He has made a way for all people to be justified "through the shedding of [Christ's] blood" (verse 25). But we must receive that gift by faith.

❖ What was the rock-bottom moment or turning point in your life when you willingly embraced the gift of salvation for your sins?

_____

_____

_____

_____

❖ What does it mean to receive Jesus' sacrifice for your sins "by faith" (verse 25)? What role does faith—trusting that God will do what he said he will do—play in your life?

_____

_____

_____

_____

Not by Works

Many of us grew up with the belief that salvation is based on a person's good behavior, adherence to rules, and spiritual pedigree. Sometimes this belief is subtle—that the good works we do as followers of Jesus will give us a slight edge in God's eyes over those who are not doing as many good deeds. Sometimes this belief is blunt—that we can actually earn God's favor by serving more, giving more, and overall *doing* more. Each path, regardless of its extreme, leads to the conclusion that salvation is based on how well we perform spiritually.

Paul exposes these kinds of beliefs as *faulty doctrine*. When he says "a person is justified by faith apart from the works of the law" (verse 28), it means that not even the best human works—nor the number of them we do—can justify us before God. Certainly, we can and should rejoice when we obey the Lord and grow in Christlikeness. However, the moment we believe our good works exert any type of obligation on God, we have moved from contentment to boasting. Our good works are the product of God's grace as his Spirit moves in us. In other words, our good works are pleasing to God—and we should strive to walk in step with God's leading—but our actions are not the pathway to salvation.

❖ Some people—perhaps unconsciously—feel they need to do good works in order to earn God's favor and approval. Why is this idea not only unbiblical but also dangerous?

_____

_____

_____

❖ Think about the idea that the good works you do are an outflowing of the grace God has been pouring into your life. How should this influence your *motives* for doing good works?

_____

_____

_____

An Example in Righteousness [Romans 4:1-25]

[1] What then shall we say that Abraham, our forefather according to the flesh, discovered in this matter? [2] If, in fact, Abraham was justified by works, he had something to boast about—but not before God. [3] What

does Scripture say? "Abraham believed God, and it was credited to him as righteousness."

[4] Now to the one who works, wages are not credited as a gift but as an obligation. [5] However, to the one who does not work but trusts God who justifies the ungodly, their faith is credited as righteousness. [6] David says the same thing when he speaks of the blessedness of the one to whom God credits righteousness apart from works:

[7] "Blessed are those
  whose transgressions are forgiven,
  whose sins are covered.
[8] Blessed is the one
  whose sin the Lord will never count against them."

[9] Is this blessedness only for the circumcised, or also for the uncircumcised? We have been saying that Abraham's faith was credited to him as righteousness. [10] Under what circumstances was it credited? Was it after he was circumcised, or before? It was not after, but before! [11] And he received circumcision as a sign, a seal of the righteousness that he had by faith while he was still uncircumcised. So then, he is the father of all who believe but have not been circumcised, in order that righteousness might be credited to them. [12] And he is then also the father of the circumcised who not only are circumcised but who also follow in the footsteps of the faith that our father Abraham had before he was circumcised.

[13] It was not through the law that Abraham and his offspring received the promise that he would be heir of the world, but through the righteousness that comes by faith. [14] For if those who depend on the law are heirs, faith means nothing and the promise is worthless, [15] because the law brings wrath. And where there is no law there is no transgression.

[16] Therefore, the promise comes by faith, so that it may be by grace and may be guaranteed to all Abraham's offspring—not only to those who are of the law but also to those who have the faith of Abraham. He is the father of us all. [17] As it is written: "I have made you a father of many

nations." He is our father in the sight of God, in whom he believed—the God who gives life to the dead and calls into being things that were not.

[18] Against all hope, Abraham in hope believed and so became the father of many nations, just as it had been said to him, "So shall your offspring be." [19] Without weakening in his faith, he faced the fact that his body was as good as dead—since he was about a hundred years old—and that Sarah's womb was also dead. [20] Yet he did not waver through unbelief regarding the promise of God, but was strengthened in his faith and gave glory to God, [21] being fully persuaded that God had power to do what he had promised. [22] This is why "it was credited to him as righteousness." [23] The words "it was credited to him" were written not for him alone, [24] but also for us, to whom God will credit righteousness—for us who believe in him who raised Jesus our Lord from the dead. [25] He was delivered over to death for our sins and was raised to life for our justification.

Original Meaning

Paul concluded his previous discussion by stressing two points. First, justification comes through God's grace, so no one can boast in their own religious accomplishments (see 3:27). Second, because of God's grace, both Jews and Gentiles have equal access to salvation (see verses 29–30). Paul will now develop these points using the story of Abraham, whom the Jews revered as a model of faithfulness to God's law.

Paul grounds his reasoning in a quote from Genesis 15:6: "Abraham believed God, and it was credited to him as righteousness" (4:3). The original Hebrew construction of this verse suggests that God's "crediting" Abraham's faith as righteous means "to account to him a righteousness that does not inherently belong to him." In other words, God granted him the *status* of righteousness because of his belief. Paul's logic is as follows: (1) When we work, an employer pays us wages as an obligation; (2) but God can never be obligated to anyone; therefore (3) God cannot credit anything to humans based on their works (see verses 4–5).

Paul then cites Psalm 32:1–2 to show that "God credits righteousness apart from works" (Romans 4:6). From the standpoint of faith, Abraham is the father of *all* who believe as he did. God's people are determined not by biological descent from Abraham but by spiritual descent from him. Gentiles who have faith can "claim" Abraham as their father. They believe, as he did, and receive, as he did, righteousness from God. Circumcision is not required to receive this gift (see verses 9–12).

Jews and Gentiles *both* benefit from God's promise made concerning Abraham's offspring. The word "offspring" (*sperma*) is important in the Genesis promise passages and in Paul's letters. The apostle uses the term to specify the two groups that make up the spiritual seed of Abraham: "those who are of the law" and "those who have the faith of Abraham" (verse 16). His concern is to show that the promise to Abraham is valid for all believers—both Jewish Christians and Gentile Christians.

Paul concludes by holding up Abraham as an example of hope (see verse 18). Abraham hoped and believed that God would give him a son. The years had passed, and starting a family at one hundred years of age made no sense. But hope in God's promise and power never left Abraham's heart. He serves as an example for believers of all generations.

❖ Who are those whom God considers to be his children? What is required for a person to become one of God's "offspring"?

Past to Present

Spiritual Apathy

We live in a time of growing apathy. In fact, a term has recently been invented to describe the presence of deep indifference in the workplace:

quiet quitting. A person who has reached this point has basically given up and is now doing the bare minimum amount of work required for the job. The person is just *phoning it in* . . . another phrase coined in the past to describe the state in which a person says, "Why bother?"

In a spiritual sense, this was happening in the hearts of some people in Paul's day. The argument went something like this: "God justifies us while we are still wicked. So why do we need to lead holy lives?" What these people were missing—and what we often miss as well—is that God's justifying the wicked cannot be viewed in isolation. God does *more* than justify us when we become Christians. He also regenerates us, sanctifies us, and causes his Spirit to indwell us. These acts of God change us from within. Given this, a genuine Christian will always reveal this transforming work of God through their obedience to God.

❖ What are some of the signs of spiritual apathy in your life?

_____

_____

_____

_____

❖ What are some of the signs of God's transforming work in your life? How has that impacted your desire to live a life pleasing to him?

_____

_____

_____

_____

Never Lose Hope

Paul writes that "against all hope, Abraham in hope believed and so became the father of many nations" (verse 18). Paul's double use of *hope* in this verse is significant. First, Abraham believed "against all hope." He trusted in God and his promises even when all the evidence went against it. Second, he believed "in hope." Abraham's faith was based on the hope that God had given him through a specific promise. This was not a blind leap in the dark. Abraham believed that God had made promises to him—and he put his hope in that fact.

It is easy for us to lose hope in our world today. When things don't go our way, we can lose hope. When we work hard but the results are not what we expected, we can lose hope. We can even lose hope when we feel that God is not responding in the way we think he should or in the timing we think he should. At such times, the enemy will whisper, "Why keep trusting in God?" But in those moments, we can look to the story of Abraham and Sarah and trust that God—"against all hope"—has not forgotten about us or the promises he has made to us.

❖ What situations in life most cause you to lose hope?

_____

_____

_____

❖ How has God given you hope? How has your hope in what Jesus did for you on the cross impacted how you view trials in life?

_____

_____

_____

Closing Prayer: God of grace, I rejoice in your generous gift of Jesus. I delight in the cleansing, deep in my soul, that Christ has purchased for me on the cross. I ask for daily reminders that I am saved by your grace, that I am sustained by your grace, and that I walk in your amazing grace. Help me to continue to grow in obedience to you and service to others as a natural outflow of the work the Holy Spirit is doing within me. In your name I pray. Amen.

4

A New Perspective on Faith

Romans 5:1–11, 12–14, 15–21

If there is an infinite and holy God, he could never love someone like me. I could never have a meaningful relationship with him. My sin is so great that there is no way the stain and punishment of it could be washed away. God would never want to work in someone like me.

These declarations have been on the lips of people throughout the centuries. Sometimes they are even articulated by faithful followers of Jesus who have read the Bible and understand what God says about salvation but wonder if it is just too good to be true. After all, the concept of God's grace *is* astounding. The almighty Creator of the universe—the one who is perfectly holy and who can tolerate no sin in his sight—willingly chooses to make a way for unrighteous sinners to not just be redeemed but also adopted into his own family.

Paul understood that many of his readers would have this same response when he spoke of God's grace. So, in this next chapter of his letter, he set about addressing these complex and critical declarations. In the process, he reveals important truths about the nature of God and why he often chooses to work in the way that he does.

Paul's words shed light on perspectives we often hold about God, faith, and ourselves that are simply incorrect. Sometimes these errors come from our life experiences. Other times the errors come through the influence of culture. There are even times when the lies of the enemy confuse our understanding when it comes to our faith. But regardless of the source, God wants to give us—through the words of Paul—a fresh new perspective on *what* we believe and *who* we actually follow.

Christ Died for the Ungodly [Romans 5:1-11]

[1] Therefore, since we have been justified through faith, we have peace with God through our Lord Jesus Christ, [2] through whom we have gained access by faith into this grace in which we now stand. And we boast in the hope of the glory of God. [3] Not only so, but we also glory in our sufferings, because we know that suffering produces perseverance; [4] perseverance, character; and character, hope. [5] And hope does not put us to shame, because God's love has been poured out into our hearts through the Holy Spirit, who has been given to us.

[6] You see, at just the right time, when we were still powerless, Christ died for the ungodly. [7] Very rarely will anyone die for a righteous person, though for a good person someone might possibly dare to die. [8] But God demonstrates his own love for us in this: While we were still sinners, Christ died for us.

[9] Since we have now been justified by his blood, how much more shall we be saved from God's wrath through him! [10] For if, while we were God's enemies, we were reconciled to him through the death of his Son, how much more, having been reconciled, shall we be saved through his life! [11] Not only is this so, but we also boast in God through our Lord Jesus Christ, through whom we have now received reconciliation.

Original Meaning

So far, Paul has focused on how God invites people—Jew and Gentile alike—to believe in Christ and enter into a relationship with him. Now he turns his attention to what comes *after* a person's justification. Paul begins by elaborating on the status of righteousness that God gives us in Christ, beginning with the fact we have "peace with God" (verse 1).

The term "peace" (*eirene*) is a rich biblical word. The Old Testament concept of peace (*shalom*) represents an objective state of harmony with God—a state that believers can now enjoy. We also gain "access by faith into this grace in which we now stand" (verse 2). Paul's use of "grace" here also refers to a state in which a believer lives. When we are justified, we are lavished with grace upon grace. God continues to pour out undeserved mercy, unexpected joy, and unyielding goodness over us.

As a result, we can "boast in the hope of the glory of God" (verse 2). The verb Paul uses for "boast" (*kauchaomai*) suggests both the idea of taking confidence in and of rejoicing in. We not only boast in God's glory but also "glory [*kauchaomai*] in our sufferings" (verse 3). In this way, Paul acknowledges that Christians *will* suffer at times—but that life's difficulties do not contradict what he has been saying about the wonderful blessings of being a Christian. God can actually use our sufferings to grow our faith (see verses 3–5).

Paul provides further proof of God's love by noting that Jesus died for us while we were still "ungodly" (verse 6). The awesome quality of God's love for us is seen in that Christ died for us while we were "still sinners" (verse 8)—while we were hating God and in rebellion against him. For this reason, Paul asserts, we can be sure of our salvation. After all, it is the "easier" thing for God to do—to deliver from his wrath those whom he has already brought to himself.

❖ What does Paul say about suffering? What are some of the traits that persevering through trials will produce in your life?

Past to Present

Consider what this passage meant to the original readers and how it applies to us today.

A Proper Perspective on Suffering

No one travels very far down the road of life without confronting suffering. We live in a broken world where pain and loss are just a part of the human experience. No one is immune. The Bible is filled with stories of God's people who faced at least some kind of pain. Paul, for his part, endured persecution, beatings, and rejection by his own people—and he was following the will of God! Living for Jesus does not guarantee a spiritual buffer from suffering. In fact, Jesus stated that following him meant taking up a cross (see Luke 14:27).

Given this reality, how *should* we respond to the trials that come our way? Paul advises that we recognize God will often use them to produce *perseverance* in our lives. Perseverance, in turn, will produce *character*—spiritual maturity in Christ—and that will lead to *hope*. When we recognize we have hope, then we can truly rejoice even in the midst of our trials and suffering, because we trust that God is at work even in these evil things to bring us blessing. Paradoxically, Paul claims we can actually "glory" in our sufferings, knowing that just as resistance to a muscle strengthens it, so challenges in our lives can strengthen us.

❖ Think of a time when you faced a difficult trial and held on to Jesus throughout that season. How did you witness your character grow as a result of that experience?

_____

_____

_____

_____

❖ What is a struggle that someone you love is facing right now? How can you encourage and support that person through this time?

_____

_____

_____

_____

A Proper Perspective on Hope

When we think of the things we hope for in life, what we often are doing is considering our wishes. We *hope* we will receive that scholarship. We *hope* the weather will be good for the party. We *hope* that person will call us back. All of these "hopes" are uncertain. In some cases, we will get what we want. In other cases, we will be disappointed by the result.

This is *not* the kind of hope that we have in Christ. When God says those who put their faith in Jesus will receive salvation and live eternally with him, it is not just wishful thinking. Paul makes an interesting statement to support this truth: "When we were still powerless, Christ died for the ungodly" (verse 6). God, through the death of Christ, justified us and reconciled us to himself even though we were still sinners. Given this incredible act of love, is there really any doubt that he will save those whom he has already reconciled to himself?

❖ Describe a time you experienced the love of God in a deep and very personal way. What was it that led to this awareness and personal confidence that you were loved by God?

_____

_____

_____

_____

❖ God's love for you is based on the rock-solid work of Jesus before his coming to earth, during his life on earth, at his sacrificial death, and even today. What are some of the things Jesus has done that assure you of the unshakable love of God?

A Proper Perspective on Justification

Paul interchanges *justify* and *reconcile* in this passage, but the terms do not mean the same thing. Rather, they are two ways of describing what happens when God first accepts us at our salvation. The Lord *justifies* us by declaring us innocent and absolving us from the punishment of our sins. He also *reconciles* us by removing the hostility that existed between us and him because of our sin. Justification is a *judicial* idea. It provides a reason why a judge (in this case, God) ruled a certain way. Reconciliation is a *relational* idea. It describes the process of restoring a relationship after an injury (in this case, a sin) has been committed.

Jesus not only took the judgment we deserved but also brought us back into harmony with God. We are deemed innocent before the holy God of heaven . . . and the guilt of our sin is removed "as far as the east is from the west" (Psalm 103:12). At the same time, we are now brought back into a right relationship with God. All animosity, conflict, and judgment were nailed to the cross with Jesus, and we can approach God knowing that nothing stands between us and our Maker.

❖ What does it mean that God justifies you? How do you respond to the idea that you are declared *innocent* of all charges before him because of your faith in Christ?

❖ What does it mean that God has reconciled you to himself? What steps are you taking to actively strengthen the relationship that you have with him?

_____

_____

_____

_____

Sin and Death [Romans 5:12-14]

[12] Therefore, just as sin entered the world through one man, and death through sin, and in this way death came to all people, because all sinned—

[13] To be sure, sin was in the world before the law was given, but sin is not charged against anyone's account where there is no law. [14] Nevertheless, death reigned from the time of Adam to the time of Moses, even over those who did not sin by breaking a command, as did Adam, who is a pattern of the one to come.

Original Meaning

The "therefore" at the beginning of this section would normally indicate Paul is summarizing what he just taught. However, what he seems to actually be doing here is providing the *basis* for what he taught in verses 1–11: Our hope of sharing God's glory is certain because we are in Christ, who has guaranteed life for us. Adam's fall introduced sin into the world, and death came as a result of that sin. Death is universal because all people have sinned. It is both physical and spiritual: separation from the body and estrangement from God.

Many Jews believed there could be no sin or death apart from the law (before the law was given). Paul, anticipating this argument, states that sin *did* exist before the Mosaic law was given and that people who lived during that time *were* condemned for their sin. The presence of positive law turns sin into "transgression" (*parabasis*). Sin may not be charged to one's individual account apart from law, but sin is still sin and brings God's condemnation and wrath.

Once again, Paul is pointing out that the law helps us recognize our need for deliverance from the destructive consequences of our spiritual rebellion. When this truth settles into our heart, we become thankful for this message that warns us of our impending demise. Just as a surgeon's diagnosis of an illness is never met with a joyful response, so we do not celebrate when sin is brought into the light. However, when we realize the diagnosis paves the way for the cure, we become thankful for both the message and the messenger.

❖ How does Paul respond to the belief that there can be no sin or death apart from the law?

_____

_____

_____

_____

Past to Present

Universality of Sin

When we read the story of Adam's sin and the consequence of death that came as a result, we might find it unfair or even abhorrent that one man's transgression thousands of years ago could determine our eternal destiny. Yet what we tend to miss is that *Adam* means "man" or "human being." In fact, translators have difficulty in deciding what occurrences of the Hebrew word (*adam*) in Genesis should translate to "man" and which to the proper name "Adam."

What this reveals is that woven into the very fabric of the Genesis narrative is the idea that Adam represents more than just an isolated individual. He is, in a sense, representative of "man" or all humanity.

Given this, when God warns the "man" that he will die if he eats from the tree of the knowledge of good and evil, a warning of *universal* death could well be intended. We are all responsible for our own choices. While Adam's sin brought about the original curse of death, *we* make the choice to sin and, as a result, incur that same penalty.

❖ How do you react to this idea that one man's sin brought about the curse of physical and spiritual death for all people? Does this seem unfair to you? Explain your response.

_____

_____

_____

_____

❖ In what ways does Adam represent all people's proclivity to sin? Why do you think it is so difficult in this world to resist the temptation to sin and so easy to disobey God?

_____

_____

_____

_____

God's Word Identifies Sin

Putting anything or anyone above God. Blaspheming the name of God. Not honoring the Lord's commands (such as observing the Sabbath as a day of rest). Disrespecting your parents and those whom God has put in authority over you. Committing murder. Engaging in adultery or sexual immorality. Stealing . . . lying . . . and coveting someone else's spouse or possessions. All of these, according to the Ten Commandments (see Exodus 20:2–17), are considered sin.

Sometimes sin is big, bold, and obvious. Other times, it comes in tiny packages. A lie told to "protect" another person. A few office

51

supplies taken from work for personal use. An extra-long glance at an attractive neighbor accompanied by lustful thoughts. A quick gossip-filled story shared with a friend. The law of God, Paul argues, reveals that these actions (and others) are to be considered *sin*, regardless of whether we might consider them to be great or small. God's Word enables us to recognize *sin* for what it is and instructs us how to avoid it.

❖ What are some of the "little" sins that people tend to justify? What is the danger in assuming God overlooks these types of sins?

❖ When has the Bible revealed a sin that you were committing? How did what you read encourage you to repent of that sin and seek God's forgiveness?

Similar and Different [Romans 5:15–21]

[15] But the gift is not like the trespass. For if the many died by the trespass of the one man, how much more did God's grace and the gift that came by the grace of the one man, Jesus Christ, overflow to the many! [16] Nor can the gift of God be compared with the result of one man's sin: The judgment followed one sin and brought condemnation, but the gift followed many trespasses and brought justification. [17] For if, by the trespass

of the one man, death reigned through that one man, how much more will those who receive God's abundant provision of grace and of the gift of righteousness reign in life through the one man, Jesus Christ!

[18] Consequently, just as one trespass resulted in condemnation for all people, so also one righteous act resulted in justification and life for all people. [19] For just as through the disobedience of the one man the many were made sinners, so also through the obedience of the one man the many will be made righteous.

[20] The law was brought in so that the trespass might increase. But where sin increased, grace increased all the more, [21] so that, just as sin reigned in death, so also grace might reign through righteousness to bring eternal life through Jesus Christ our Lord.

Original Meaning

Paul concluded verse 14 by stating Adam was a "pattern of the one to come"; that is, of Christ. However, before he pursues the similarity between the two, he will first note some of the differences. These differences boil down to one important truth: In Christ, God deals with people on the basis of grace. The word *grace* and the related term *gift* occur eight times in verses 15–17. What happened as a result of Adam's sin was entirely a matter of consequences. Death, judgment, and condemnation inevitably and justly followed Adam's sin.

What has happened as a result of Christ is quite different. In place of condemnation, Jesus has brought *justification*. Death reigned because of Adam's sin, but life now reigns because of Christ. We see in this, Paul concludes, evidence of the overwhelming grace of God. God's grace operating through the work of Christ means there is a "much more" quality in what Jesus has accomplished in comparison to what Adam had done. Jesus does more than just cancel the effects of Adam's sin; he also enables those who receive the "abundant provision of grace" and "the gift of righteousness" to actually "reign in life" (verse 17).

Paul continues in verses 18–21 to contrast what Adam did with what Christ did. Adam committed "one trespass" by disobeying God; Christ committed "one righteous act" by obeying God. (Paul here is likely thinking of a single manifestation of Jesus' obedience to his Father—submitting to God's will to die on a cross.) Adam turned away from God and violated his command; Jesus turned toward God and did the will of his Father. Because of Adam's sin, many people were inaugurated into a state of sinfulness; because of Christ's obedience, many people have now been appointed to a status of righteousness.

❖ What does it mean that Adam was a "pattern" of the one to come? What is the major difference between Adam and Jesus that Paul points out in this passage?

Past to Present

Impact of Sin

Imagine you live in a house with a leaky roof. Every time it rains, the water seeps through the ceiling and creates a puddle on the floor below. You know you should fix the roof . . . but you decide the problem isn't that bad and it's not impacting anyone else. All the while, the leak is creating mildew and black mold that is hazardous to the other people living in your home.

Sin is a bit like this leaky roof. We may think it just impacts us, but the truth is it affects other people in our lives. Sin can break trust, cause divisions, and destroy bonds. It can lead to feelings of guilt, anger, and shame that cause us to lash out. It can create patterns of behavior that are passed on to future generations. As Paul notes, Adam's one trespass "resulted in condemnation for all people" (verse 18). We need to consider the impact of our sin!

❖ What are some of the ways you have seen that one person's sin can directly and negatively impact another person?

_____

_____

_____

_____

_____

❖ Why do you think people tend to underestimate the impact of their sins? Why is it important to be clearheaded about how your sin is impacting others?

_____

_____

_____

_____

_____

Impact of Grace

Picture yourself sitting on your couch when the doorbell rings. When you go to the door, you find a well-dressed man standing there with an envelope in his hand. He informs you that he works for a law firm and one of his wealthy clients has left you a great deal of money. All you have to do is sign a few forms and the cash is yours. How would you respond? Well, if you are like most people, you would certainly question whether all this was too good to be true. People just don't leave money to people they don't know. You would likely conclude this was a scam.

When it comes to God's grace, we might respond in the same way. The greatness of our sin is real. God's judgment against us is justified.

The penalty of our sin is death. Can we really believe that God willingly sent his Son to die in our place so our sins could be forgiven? It all seems too good to be true. Yet this is precisely what Paul argues that Christ did on our behalf: "Just as one trespass resulted in condemnation for all people, so also one righteous act resulted in justification and life for all people" (verse 18). Jesus, by dying on the cross for our sins, has provided a way for us to be reconciled with God. This is the impact of grace!

❖ In what ways have you wrestled with the concern that God's gift of grace—of eternal salvation in Christ—is just "too good to be true"?

_____

_____

_____

_____

_____

❖ Why do you think people often feel their sin is too great—or they have done too much wrong in their lives—for God to forgive them?

_____

_____

_____

_____

_____

Closing Prayer: God of truth, I confess that my mind can drift from your truth. The lies of this world and the enemy can taint my thinking. Give me fresh perspective that is in line with your Word. Let the message of your grace lock in my mind and fill my heart. Help me see myself, other people, and you through the lens of your Word. For the glory of Jesus. Amen!

5

From Death to Life

Romans 6:1-10, 11-14, 15-23

The word *metamorphosis* describes a radical transformation. It is most strikingly seen in the way a caterpillar transforms into a butterfly. Caterpillars hatch from eggs laid on leaves. The caterpillar eats and eats, splitting its skin and shedding it around four to five times. Caterpillars can grow to one hundred times their original size during this stage.

When the caterpillar is full-grown, it stops eating and builds a protective coating known as a *chrysalis*. In this transition stage, special cells activate that form the adult butterfly's legs, wings, eyes, and other parts. Around eight to fourteen days later, the butterfly emerges from the chrysalis fully formed—and looking completely different from its caterpillar state. There is a connection, but the butterfly appears entirely different. In its former state it could only crawl, but now it can fly.

We undergo a spiritual metamorphosis when we come to faith in Christ. We put to death our old "caterpillar" state and begin a new life in our "butterfly" stage. Whereas before we were bound to the ways and whims of the world, we now find freedom, life, purpose, and hope. Jesus takes us from the depths of the grave to the heights of heaven.

When Paul paints this vivid picture of a believer's metamorphosis in Romans, he is not merely presenting an image but also making a declaration. Through faith in Christ, we *die* to our old life and slavery to sin. The power of the grave and the enemy no longer have dominion over us. The pathway set by Adam is overcome and a new one is given to us in Christ. Righteousness is not just a suggestion, goal, or good idea . . . it must rule our lives. The journey to and with Jesus is one that leads us from death to life in more ways than we comprehend.

United with Jesus in Death and Life [Romans 6:1-10]

[1] What shall we say, then? Shall we go on sinning so that grace may increase? [2] By no means! We are those who have died to sin; how can we live in it any longer? [3] Or don't you know that all of us who were baptized into Christ Jesus were baptized into his death? [4] We were therefore buried with him through baptism into death in order that, just as Christ was raised from the dead through the glory of the Father, we too may live a new life.

[5] For if we have been united with him in a death like his, we will certainly also be united with him in a resurrection like his. [6] For we know that our old self was crucified with him so that the body ruled by sin might be done away with, that we should no longer be slaves to sin— [7] because anyone who has died has been set free from sin.

[8] Now if we died with Christ, we believe that we will also live with him. [9] For we know that since Christ was raised from the dead, he cannot die again; death no longer has mastery over him. [10] The death he died, he died to sin once for all; but the life he lives, he lives to God.

Original Meaning

Paul begins by saying believers are those "who have died to sin" (verse 2). This powerful image depicts a dramatic and decisive shift in our state of being. When we accept Christ as our Savior, we "die" to sin and its hold over us. We might not see this change immediately, because we still live in a sin-stained world, but it has taken place.

Paul goes on to describe how this transfer from our former state of sin to our new life in Christ has taken place. In baptism, we are joined to Christ and to his death and resurrection (see verses 3–5). Jesus' own death was a death "to sin," and his resurrection meant living "to God" (verse 10). Therefore, those who *participate* in Christ's death and resurrection have also died to sin and now live to God. When we place our faith in Jesus, his death and resurrection become our own. Baptism is thus symbolic of our whole conversion experience. We are brought into union with Jesus and the powerful events of his redemptive work.

Paul uses a future tense to describe our participation in Christ's resurrection: "we will . . . be united with him" (verse 5). While we experience new life when we come to Christ, Paul is likely referring here to the promise of our future resurrection—when we are raised with Christ at his second coming. The statement Paul makes to describe what Jesus accomplished in his death and resurrection is thus more than just a picture of what our Savior has done. It serves as a promise of our freedom from sin and assurance of our future resurrection.

❖ According to Paul, how does your outlook on sin and your view of yourself change when you come to faith in Jesus?

_____

_____

_____

_____

Past to Present

Consider what this passage meant to the original readers and how it applies to us today.

Dying with Christ
When we place our faith in Jesus, everything changes. Of course, this process takes time. We will still stumble and be tempted at times to not trust that God's grace is sufficient. But our desires begin to change. The

taste of sinful practices starts to leave a bitter taste in our mouths. The false pleasures we once pursued suddenly feel hollow. We are no longer slaves to sin but are free to live in ways that honor our Maker.

This is the journey of dying to sin so we can be set free from sin. When we were "baptized into Christ Jesus" we were also "baptized into his death" (verse 3). The death and resurrection of Jesus—the sacrifice for our sins that we have accepted—have broken the bonds that once held us. Our part now is to receive the help of the Holy Spirit and reject the enticements of the enemy. We *can* say no to sin. We *can* reject past patterns of compromise. We *are* empowered to live a new kind of life.

❖ What are some of the desires that changed in your life as you have grown in spiritual maturity and continued to follow after Christ?

❖ What is one area in which the Holy Spirit has helped you to resist the enemy? What is one area in which you still struggle?

Raised with Christ

Paul says we were "buried with [Jesus]" so that "just as Christ was raised from the dead . . . we too may live a new life" (verse 4). Jesus, though sinless, took on flesh to identify with us. He was subject to the power of sin and "tempted in every way, just as we are" (Hebrews 4:15). In this sense, Jesus, too, needed to die to sin's power. He accomplished this when he rose on the third day, breaking the power of sin, hell, and death.

FROM DEATH TO LIFE

Spiritual *life* is the result of identifying with Jesus' resurrection and likewise putting sin to *death*. Jesus' victory over the grave means he now lives in a state in which "death no longer has mastery over him" (Romans 6:9). Jesus has conquered death and, Paul implies, those who belong to him also have the assurance of conquering death. The risen Christ is alive and dwells in us. Sin no longer has mastery over us. We are spiritually alive and can walk in the power of Jesus' resurrection.

❖ You were "buried" with Christ when you put your faith in him. How has Jesus helped you to "die" to sin's power?

_____

_____

_____

_____

❖ What does it mean to you that the risen Christ is alive and "dwells" within you? What hope does knowing this truth give you today?

_____

_____

_____

_____

Faith in Action [Romans 6:11–14]

[11] In the same way, count yourselves dead to sin but alive to God in Christ Jesus. [12] Therefore do not let sin reign in your mortal body so that you obey its evil desires. [13] Do not offer any part of yourself to sin as an instrument of wickedness, but rather offer yourselves to God as those who have been brought from death to life; and offer every part of yourself to him as an instrument of righteousness. [14] For sin shall no longer be your master, because you are not under the law, but under grace.

Original Meaning

A common pattern that Paul employs in his letters is to first tell his readers *about* a spiritual truth and then relate how they should *respond* to it. We would expect this same pattern to follow here. However, what we find in verse 11 is more of an intermediate step—a way for readers to come to grips with what Paul has been teaching. Only by *continually* (the Greek verb is in the present tense) looking at ourselves as people who have truly died to sin and been made alive in Christ will we be able to live out the new status that God has given us.

Paul then moves into the realm of action in verses 12–13. Because of our new state in Christ, we are to not allow sin to "reign" or "obey its evil desires." In other words, we take *possession* of the victory that Jesus has won for us over sin. We no longer allow sin to use our various capacities and abilities as an "instrument of wickedness" but willingly place those things at the disposal of God, our new master, to make into an "instrument of righteousness."

Paul concludes with one more reminder of how we should respond to the new life we have been given in Christ: "Sin shall no longer be [our] master" (verse 14). Paul then emphasizes that our freedom from sin's power is a continuing state we can look forward to enjoying forever, because we are "not under the law, but under grace." We now stand under the new covenant of grace, and the law of the old covenant no longer has direct control over us. God's grace dominates the new regime in our lives that was inaugurated by Jesus.

❖ Paul gives three exhortations using the word *offer.* What are followers of Jesus called *to* offer or *not* offer according to this passage?

Past to Present

Living in Freedom

People who have been put in jail for committing a misdemeanor look forward to the day when they will be released. The days and weeks they spend separated from their loved ones—and from society at large—give them time to ponder the mistakes they have made. Those who are wise also consider what changes they need to make to ensure they will not end up in jail again. After all, living in freedom requires following certain rules that society puts in place.

Paul writes that Jesus has set us free from the "jail" of our past lives when sin was our master. Now, we "are not under the law, but under grace" (verse 14). Jesus has effectively opened the door of our cell and guided us to the front entrance so we can live in freedom. However, maintaining that freedom requires us to not allow sin to "reign in [our] mortal body" (verse 12). Just as a person freed from jail must "put to death" past behaviors that led to them getting locked up, so we must put to death any behaviors that led to us being slaves to sin.

❖ What does it mean to not allow sin to reign in your body? What actions does it take on your part to ensure this does not happen?

_____

_____

_____

_____

❖ What does it mean to live in the freedom that Jesus provides? What do you most appreciate about that freedom you now enjoy?

_____

_____

_____

_____

Role of Baptism

Paul refers to water baptism as representing the point at which a person is joined with Christ. We are "baptized into Christ" (verse 3) and "buried with him through baptism" (verse 4), which enables us to count ourselves "dead to sin" (verse 11). Given this, it is important to consider the role that water baptism plays in our faith.

Baptism is public declaration of our faith in Christ. It identifies us as "Christians" to others and indicates our intent to follow Jesus. While baptism does not symbolize our being buried with Christ, it is the means through which we were identified with him. The New Testament writers present water baptism as one component of a larger experience of "conversion-initiation"—with the others being faith, repentance, and the gift of the Holy Spirit. This broader New Testament context helps us conclude that when Paul refers to baptism in Romans 6, he intends to include faith, repentance, and the gift of the Spirit.

Baptism is an important part of our conversion experience. It sets a "seal" on our experience. Paul is clear that a person becomes a Christian by believing in the Lord Jesus. However, were we to ask him about an "unbaptized believer," he would likely respond, "Yes, such a person is saved. But why in the world isn't that person baptized?"

❖ If someone were to ask what it means to be baptized and what difference it makes, how would you respond?

❖ What role do you think baptism plays in a believer's life? If you have been baptized, what did the experience mean to you? Why is it important to reflect on your baptism and remember that moment in your faith journey?

_____

_____

_____

_____

A New Allegiance [Romans 6:15–23]

¹⁵ What then? Shall we sin because we are not under the law but under grace? By no means! ¹⁶ Don't you know that when you offer yourselves to someone as obedient slaves, you are slaves of the one you obey—whether you are slaves to sin, which leads to death, or to obedience, which leads to righteousness? ¹⁷ But thanks be to God that, though you used to be slaves to sin, you have come to obey from your heart the pattern of teaching that has now claimed your allegiance. ¹⁸ You have been set free from sin and have become slaves to righteousness.

¹⁹ I am using an example from everyday life because of your human limitations. Just as you used to offer yourselves as slaves to impurity and to ever-increasing wickedness, so now offer yourselves as slaves to righteousness leading to holiness. ²⁰ When you were slaves to sin, you were free from the control of righteousness. ²¹ What benefit did you reap at that time from the things you are now ashamed of? Those things result in death! ²² But now that you have been set free from sin and have become slaves of God, the benefit you reap leads to holiness, and the result is eternal life. ²³ For the wages of sin is death, but the gift of God is eternal life in Christ Jesus our Lord.

Original Meaning

Paul began Romans 6 with a key question for his readers: "Shall we go on sinning so that grace may increase?" (verse 1). He now returns to that theme, asking his readers, "What then? Shall we sin because we are not under the law but under grace?" (verse 15). Once again, his answer to his own question is the same: "By no means!" (verses 2, 15).

Paul understands his claim that believers have been transferred from the regime of the Mosaic law to the regime of grace could lead some to think that sin does not matter. He refutes this idea by employing "an example from everyday life" (verse 19)—slavery—to show the fallacy of such thinking. His contention is that we become slaves to whatever we obey. If we obey sin, we become "slaves to sin"—and the result is death. If we obey God, we become slaves "to obedience"—which leads to righteousness (verse 16). As followers of Jesus, Paul asserts, we have made the choice to "become slaves to righteousness" (verse 18).

In our former state, we had a false sense of "freedom" in that we were free to sin but not to lead a righteous life. This kind of freedom only resulted in behavior that ends in death. But in our new state in Christ, we have the freedom to lead a righteous life—which leads to holiness and *eternal* life. Paul sums up these ideas with another common illustration of his day: *earnings*. He writes, "The wages of sin is death, but the gift of God is eternal life in Christ Jesus our Lord" (verse 23).

❖ What kind of "slave" were you before you followed Jesus? What kind of "slave" are you now after placing your faith in the Savior?

Past to Present

Slaves to Sin

In 1979, Bob Dylan released a song titled "Gotta Serve Somebody." In the opening lines of the song, Dylan describes people from different walks of life: ambassadors, gamblers, dancers, heavyweight boxing champions, and wealthy socialites. He then introduces the theme that runs throughout it: "You're gonna have to serve somebody." Dylan states who you serve "may be the devil" or "may be the Lord." But, no matter who you are, you *will* serve somebody.

Dylan was captivated by the idea that everyone is a servant (or slave) to something (or someone). This message resonates with what Paul is expressing in this section of Romans. He states there are two options for us as human beings. We can choose to be either a slave to sin or a bondservant of Jesus and his righteousness. For this reason, we are wise to ask, "Am I living as a person surrendered to the will of Jesus or to the enticements of this world?"

❖ What does it look like to be a slave to sin? What reasons does Paul give as to why you should not choose to sin just so you can experience more of God's grace?

_____

_____

_____

_____

❖ What does it mean to be a slave to righteousness? How does surrendering to God's will help you to avoid the enticements of this world?

_____

_____

_____

_____

Slaves to Holiness

The 1998 movie *The Truman Show* provides an illustration of some peoples' lives. In the film, Truman Burbank believed he was living a free life, but in reality every situation he faced was carefully scripted and broadcast to the world. Truman thought his choices were his own, but his every move was manipulated by the show's producer.

Those who choose not to follow Christ often pride themselves on being "free." Paul agrees they do have a freedom—the freedom *not* to be able to lead righteous lives. These individuals, by determining not to follow Jesus, are being manipulated by the enemy and are in bondage to sin, with the result of such freedom being death. However, those who follow Jesus experience a freedom that leads to holiness, "and the result is eternal life" (verse 22).

❖ What are some of the ways the enemy likes to manipulate people into thinking they are free when they are actually under his control and in bondage to sin?

_____

_____

_____

_____

❖ What does Paul mean when he says that the "wages of sin is death" (verse 23)? What are people who continue to willfully engage in sin "earning" for themselves?

_____

_____

_____

_____

_____

Closing Prayer: *Lord God, please remind me, each day, that I am free from the bondage of sin and am called to a life of surrender to your will. Thank you for destroying the power of sin and the grip of the enemy. I bow my knees to you and long to be fully yielded to what is good, beautiful, and honoring to you. Help me to choose to pursue your righteousness. Amen.*

6

Faith, Freedom, and Fruitfulness

Romans 7:1-6, 7-12, 13-25

It's a battle that rages every day in households around the world. A parent bakes a batch of hot, gooey, delicious chocolate-chip cookies and places them on the kitchen counter to cool. "Now, those are for later," the parent says to the eager-eyed children who suddenly appear. "Dinner is in less than an hour, and I don't want you to spoil your appetite. Those are for dessert."

What will the children do in this instance? They have been given a "law" by their parent. They understand that breaking that law comes with consequences. They might even recognize the law has been made with their best interests in mind. Still . . . those cookies smell so good! The temptation to grab one off the counter feels overwhelming. Rationalization soon sets in. *Maybe I can get away with sneaking just a little nibble off the corner of one.*

As Paul has stated in Romans, the law of God makes us aware of how often we fall into sin. In his words, "through the law we become conscious of our sin" (3:20). No one, except Jesus, has ever perfectly kept God's law—we have all succumbed to the temptation to "take a bite of the cookie." Given all this, the message that Paul delivers next should serve as a great encouragement to us and give us hope.

What is this message? Simply that Christians do not live under the law! When we chose to die with Christ, we also died to the law. We are now slaves of righteousness and live under a system of *grace*. Of course, this does not mean we also died to good works—something Paul is careful to point out. God wants us to lead righteous lives. The difference is that we are no longer condemned by the law when we fail to live up to God's standard. We have been delivered "through Jesus Christ our Lord" (7:25). When we recognize this truth—that we are no longer *bound* by the law—we grow in our desire to surrender to the will of God.

Free at Last [Romans 7:1-6]

[1] Do you not know, brothers and sisters—for I am speaking to those who know the law—that the law has authority over someone only as long as that person lives? [2] For example, by law a married woman is bound to her husband as long as he is alive, but if her husband dies, she is released from the law that binds her to him. [3] So then, if she has sexual relations with another man while her husband is still alive, she is called an adulteress. But if her husband dies, she is released from that law and is not an adulteress if she marries another man.

[4] So, my brothers and sisters, you also died to the law through the body of Christ, that you might belong to another, to him who was raised from the dead, in order that we might bear fruit for God. [5] For when we were in the realm of the flesh, the sinful passions aroused by the law were at work in us, so that we bore fruit for death. [6] But now, by dying to what once bound us, we have been released from the law so that we serve in the new way of the Spirit, and not in the old way of the written code.

Original Meaning

Paul has stressed the negative effect of the Mosaic law throughout Romans. He now adds a twist to his argument, stating that just as

Christians have died to sin, so they also have died to the binding authority of the law. Paul's presiding principle is "the law has authority over someone only as long as that person lives" (verse 1). By way of example, he states that when the husband of a married woman dies, she is no longer bound to him under the law. In the same way, the law has no binding effect over Christians, who have put sin to death.

Such a death brings freedom from the law. However, Paul points out that it also leads to a new relationship. As followers of Jesus, we have experienced a death in our relationship to the law, which enables us to enter into a new relationship with Christ. We have thus not only been released from bondage to *sin* but also been released from bondage to the *law*. This release was accomplished through Jesus' death on the cross.

What lies in the background of Paul's teaching is his concept of salvation-history. The era of the law had come to an end with the redemptive work of Christ. Given this reality, it is nonsensical for us as followers of Jesus to say that we are still under the law. In fact, to do so is to effectively deny that Jesus brought about the end of the law. We have now been joined to Christ so we can "bear fruit for God" (verse 4). The Mosaic law, written on stone tablets, cannot change the human heart. Only the Spirit of God can accomplish this in our lives.

❖ Paul uses the word *law* several times in this passage. What extent does Paul say the authority of the law has over a person? What releases a person from the law?

_____

_____

_____

_____

_____

_____

_____

Past to Present

Consider what this passage meant to the original readers and how it applies to us today.

Released from the Law

As modern readers, we might find it strange that Paul devotes so much time in Romans to explaining how the Mosaic law no longer has authority over a believer's life. However, we have to remember this was a great theological debate in his day. The earliest Christians were primarily Jews who recognized Jesus as the Messiah in fulfillment of Old Testament prophecies. Many of these Jewish believers were wondering if the law still had a role to play in their lives. Should they still be trying to follow the law? Or should the law be rejected completely?

Paul's central claim is that believers have been *released* from the law. He has already argued that a person who decides to follow Jesus has been "buried with him through baptism into death" (6:4). Now he adds that the law has authority over someone "only as long as that person lives" (7:1). The connection is that a believer has "died to the law" (verse 4) and thus the law no longer has *any* authority over him or her. As we all know, laws in our modern society do not apply to *dead* people. In the same way, we are considered "dead" when it comes to the hold that the Mosaic law has over our lives. We have been released from the law.

❖ Why is it important to recognize that obedience to the law is not your source of salvation? How do you respond to the heartbeat of the two paragraphs above?

_____

_____

_____

_____

❖ If you grew up in a legalistic context (in the church, another religious system, or maybe a family system), how did that rule-centered and rigid setting stifle your freedom in Christ and center your life on rules, regulations, and performance?

_____

_____

_____

_____

Bearing Fruit for God

When you are planting a garden, the goal is for it to produce something useful. You want the seeds you are putting in the soil to grow into plants that produce lettuce, carrots, tomatoes, or whatever else you want to harvest. It is not enough to just bring "death" to the weeds that threaten to choke out the plants. You want something to grow where that space was made. Plants have to be productive and yield a crop.

The same is true of the Christian life. Followers of Jesus have "died to the law," and this death occurred so you "might belong to another" and ultimately "bear fruit for God" (verse 4). In other words, the fact that you have died to the law and now belong to Christ means your life should produce fruit for him. What is this fruit? In another letter, Paul provides nine qualities: "love, joy, peace, forbearance, kindness, goodness, faithfulness, gentleness and self-control" (Galatians 5:22–23). When you exhibit this kind of fruit in your life, it is an indication you are now operating "in the new way of the Spirit" (Romans 7:6).

❖ When you think of your life in Christ as a garden, what kinds of "seeds" are you planting in the soil of your heart and mind?

_____

_____

_____

_____

❖ What is some of the "fruit" that you can say with confidence that your life is producing for God? What kind of fruit do you most want to produce?

_____

_____

_____

_____

_____

The Law and Sin [Romans 7:7-12]

⁷ What shall we say, then? Is the law sinful? Certainly not! Nevertheless, I would not have known what sin was had it not been for the law. For I would not have known what coveting really was if the law had not said, "You shall not covet." ⁸ But sin, seizing the opportunity afforded by the commandment, produced in me every kind of coveting. For apart from the law, sin was dead. ⁹ Once I was alive apart from the law; but when the commandment came, sin sprang to life and I died. ¹⁰ I found that the very commandment that was intended to bring life actually brought death. ¹¹ For sin, seizing the opportunity afforded by the commandment, deceived me, and through the commandment put me to death. ¹² So then, the law is holy, and the commandment is holy, righteous and good.

Original Meaning

Paul anticipates an objection at this point to his presentation of the gospel. He understands that some might imply from his statements that the law is sin—an evil thing. However, if this were the case, it would forfeit any claim the gospel is the fulfillment of the Old Testament. Rather, the law is *not* sin, though it is true the law and sin *are* related.

Paul explains that he came to know sin through the law. As an illustration, he uses the tenth commandment. The Mosaic law helped him to understand that he should not covet and to know the extent and seriousness of such sin. However, taking the argument one step further, he notes that he not only came to know sin through the law but also was led into greater sinning through that same law. He likely has in mind the power of a prohibition to stimulate a sinful action in rebellious people. As we are only too well aware, when we are told *not* to do something, it can cause us to desire all the more to *want* to do it.

Paul likely has in mind the experience he and all Jews went through as part of the people of Israel. Jews in Paul's day had a lively sense of their involvement with the great acts in the history of Israel, so it would be natural for Paul to merge his own experience relative to sin and the law with the experience of his people. As he has made clear throughout Romans, the coming of "the commandment" (verse 9), the giving of the law of Moses, meant for Israel not life but death. It exposed and magnified the peoples' sin, and greater wrath came on them.

❖ What does Paul say the law allows you to come to understand? How does this show that the law itself is holy, righteous, and good?

_____

_____

_____

_____

_____

Past to Present

The Problem of Human Nature
Fire can be helpful and good. Turn on the burner of your kitchen stove, and you can heat up water for tea, warm up some soup, and cook all sorts of tasty meals. Fire, in that situation, is a gift. But imagine that same fire getting out of control. The oil in the frying pan bursts into flames and the fire jumps to the curtains. In a matter of seconds, the

flames that once safely cooked your food are now threatening to burn down your house. Fundamentally, the nature of the fire has not changed, but the location of the flames has made a world of difference.

The law is a bit like fire. The law of God is holy and righteous. Just as fire is good in that it enables you to cook food, so God's law is good in that it allows you to come to understand what is sin. However, at the same time, there is an aspect of your human nature that compels you to do what you are not supposed to do. In that case, the law is a bit like the fire jumping out of the frying pan to set the kitchen ablaze. As Paul writes, "the very commandment that was intended to bring life actually brought death" (verse 10). Paradoxically, the very prohibition of a sin can lead to committing even more of that same sin.

❖ How do you interpret what Paul is saying about human nature in this passage?

❖ What is an example from your life of how knowing that you *shouldn't* do something actually led to you *wanting* to do that very thing?

Impossible Without God

For years, medical professionals declared it was physiologically impossible to run a sub-four-minute mile. The claim was that the human body did not have the ability to reach the speed it would take to accomplish this feat. Then, on May 6, 1954, English athlete Roger Bannister recorded a time of 3:59.4. Today, the world record is 3:43.13, held by Hicham El Guerrouj of Morocco. In coming years, runners will certainly shave fractions of a second off this time. But this does not mean there are *no* limitations on the human body. For instance, given what we currently know about it, a sub-three-minute mile *would* be impossible.

Paul is clear there are spiritual obstacles that likewise make it impossible for human beings to do certain things. For instance, we know—based on Paul's own example—that the tenth commandment tells us it is a sin to covet (see Exodus 20:17). However, *knowing* coveting is a sin and actually *not* coveting are two very different things! The sinful condition of humanity renders it impossible for us to fully obey God's commands. We will *always* fall short of the law. Fortunately, as Jesus said, "What is impossible with man is possible with God" (Luke 18:27). The Holy Spirit, who dwells within us, sets himself against the desires of our flesh and leads us into righteousness (see Galatians 5:16–18). What is impossible for us is possible with God.

❖ What evidence have you seen that proves human beings are simply incapable of living up to God's high standards without his intervention and help?

❖ What are some practical ways the Holy Spirit has enabled you to live according to God's standards? What is an area in your life where you would like to receive more of his help?

The Battle Rages [Romans 7:13-25]

[13] Did that which is good, then, become death to me? By no means! Nevertheless, in order that sin might be recognized as sin, it used what is good to bring about my death, so that through the commandment sin might become utterly sinful.

[14] We know that the law is spiritual; but I am unspiritual, sold as a slave to sin. [15] I do not understand what I do. For what I want to do I do not do, but what I hate I do. [16] And if I do what I do not want to do, I agree that the law is good. [17] As it is, it is no longer I myself who do it, but it is sin living in me. [18] For I know that good itself does not dwell in me, that is, in my sinful nature. For I have the desire to do what is good, but I cannot carry it out. [19] For I do not do the good I want to do, but the evil I do not want to do—this I keep on doing. [20] Now if I do what I do not want to do, it is no longer I who do it, but it is sin living in me that does it.

[21] So I find this law at work: Although I want to do good, evil is right there with me. [22] For in my inner being I delight in God's law; [23] but I see another law at work in me, waging war against the law of my mind and making me a prisoner of the law of sin at work within me. [24] What a wretched man I am! Who will rescue me from this body that is subject to death? [25] Thanks be to God, who delivers me through Jesus Christ our Lord!

So then, I myself in my mind am a slave to God's law, but in my sinful nature a slave to the law of sin.

Original Meaning

Paul has been clear in Romans that one of the purposes of the Mosaic law was to enable us to identify sin in our lives. The law reveals to us what is acceptable and what is unacceptable in God's sight. Paul now expounds on this idea by drawing on an example from his own life. Scholars have debated exactly *what* experience Paul is referring to, but his main concern is to explain why the law has brought death to Israel.

The law, as Paul explained in verse 12, is spiritual—it is "holy." However, people are "unspiritual" and "sold as a slave to sin" (verse 14). Sin is not an independent entity. Rather, it exists only as we miss the mark of God's holiness . . . and then we become bound to it. We find, like Paul, that we agree with God's law in our minds but cannot actually obey it (see verses 15–20). The struggle is that the good law of God is at war with the "law of sin" (verse 23). We are held captive under the law of sin, which means we can never escape the penalty for our rebellion against God, which is death. Or, at least, we cannot do so on our own.

Paul is not saying that we have no responsibility for our actions. Rather, he is trying to explain our actions by revealing the force within us that leads us to act as we do. Just as God in his law makes a claim on our lives, so sin exerts its own claim on us. These two claims battle for our allegiance, but in the end, God's law simply does not have the power to deliver us from the power of sin. The good news is that Jesus *does* have the power to deliver us from sin. Yet the battle still rages in our hearts and minds. It did for Paul, and it will for each of us.

❖ Paul writes that in his "inner being" he delights in God's law (verse 22). What is the other "law" at work in him (see verse 23)?

_____

_____

_____

_____

_____

_____

Past to Present

Willing Versus Doing

Bernard of Clairvaux, a French theologian who lived in the mid-twelfth century, is believed to have coined the idiom, "The road to hell is paved with good intentions." Most of us have good intentions and want to do what is good, healthy, and right. We *want* to avoid eating sugary snacks. We *want* to think through our responses before lashing out in anger. We *want* to spend time with God in prayer each day. But sadly, our actions don't always follow our intent.

The delicious-looking donut we pass by in the store seems to call out to us. The family member who is always trying to provoke us makes another irritating comment. There just doesn't seem to be any time to spend with God when there are so many other things that require our attention. Our willpower in these situations (and in others) does not enable us to do what we vowed to do. It leaves us in the same predicament that Paul found himself in when he said, "For what I want to do I do not do, but what I hate I do" (verse 15).

❖ What does this battle between your will and your actions look like in your life?

_____

_____

_____

_____

_____

❖ What is one area in which your willpower is never strong enough to prevent you from doing what you don't want to do? How has God given you grace in that situation?

_____

_____

_____

_____

_____

Thanks Be to God

Paul's predicament caused him to cry out, "What a wretched man I am! Who will rescue me from this body that is subject to death?" (verse 24). We can all relate to the frustration he was feeling. We know the desperation of wanting to do good but finding evil right there beside us. Thankfully, Paul also recognized God doesn't want any of us to remain in that place. He writes, "Thanks be to God, who delivers me through Jesus Christ our Lord!" (verse 25).

This eruption of thanksgiving from Paul comes when he considers the state from which Christ has rescued him. This should be our response as well. When we battle temptation and stumble into sin, we can thank God for his grace and willingness to forgive us. When we battle temptation and come out victorious through the power of the Holy Spirit, we can thank God for his presence and deliverance. In all circumstances, we can give heartfelt thanks to God.

❖ When you consider how God has forgiven you of your sins, what expression of praise does that prompt you to want to make? Write down that prayer below.

_____

_____

_____

_____

❖ When you consider how God empowers you to resist temptation, what expression of praise does that prompt you to want to make? Write down that prayer below.

_____

_____

_____

_____

_____

Closing Prayer: God of freedom, I believe in you and have faith that you have crushed the power of sin. Please continue to help me to follow the path of righteousness that leads to life and reject the ways of this world that lead only to death. I thank and praise you for delivering me from the authority of the enemy. Thank you for giving me the victory in my life. Amen.

7

No Condemnation

Romans 8:1–13, 18–30, 31–39

Paul has established that we "all have sinned" (3:23) and "the wages of sin"—the penalty we earned for our transgressions—"is death" (6:23). Our situation is like that of a prisoner who has been condemned of committing a crime. We know God's law and even "have the desire to do what is good," but we find we "cannot carry it out" (7:18). We are therefore guilty of breaking God's law and deserving of the consequences.

However, in this next section, Paul makes the astonishing assertion that "there is now no condemnation for those who are in Christ Jesus" (8:1). It's as if we are awaiting our fate in our cell but then receive word we have been granted a full pardon. We were once *condemned* due to our sin. But now, because we have embraced the sacrifice Jesus made on our behalf and put our faith in him, we have been declared *righteous*—one who acts in accordance with God's law and is deemed free of guilt.

When Jesus began his ministry, he stated that his mission was "to proclaim freedom for the prisoners" and "set the oppressed free" (Luke 4:18). Jesus has released us from the prison of sin. He has opened the door to our jail cell and invited us to step out into the light. He has silenced the enemy's accusations against us and is now interceding on our behalf. When we understand this truth, we can boldly declare alongside Paul, "Who will bring any charge against those whom God has chosen?" (Romans 8:33). No one can condemn us if we belong to Christ!

Living in the Spirit [Romans 8:1–13]

¹ Therefore, there is now no condemnation for those who are in Christ Jesus, ² because through Christ Jesus the law of the Spirit who gives life has set you free from the law of sin and death. ³ For what the law was powerless to do because it was weakened by the flesh, God did by sending his own Son in the likeness of sinful flesh to be a sin offering. And so he condemned sin in the flesh, ⁴ in order that the righteous requirement of the law might be fully met in us, who do not live according to the flesh but according to the Spirit.

⁵ Those who live according to the flesh have their minds set on what the flesh desires; but those who live in accordance with the Spirit have their minds set on what the Spirit desires. ⁶ The mind governed by the flesh is death, but the mind governed by the Spirit is life and peace. ⁷ The mind governed by the flesh is hostile to God; it does not submit to God's law, nor can it do so. ⁸ Those who are in the realm of the flesh cannot please God.

⁹ You, however, are not in the realm of the flesh but are in the realm of the Spirit, if indeed the Spirit of God lives in you. And if anyone does not have the Spirit of Christ, they do not belong to Christ. ¹⁰ But if Christ is in you, then even though your body is subject to death because of sin, the Spirit gives life because of righteousness. ¹¹ And if the Spirit of him who raised Jesus from the dead is living in you, he who raised Christ from the dead will also give life to your mortal bodies because of his Spirit who lives in you.

¹² Therefore, brothers and sisters, we have an obligation—but it is not to the flesh, to live according to it. ¹³ For if you live according to the flesh, you will die; but if by the Spirit you put to death the misdeeds of the body, you will live.

Original Meaning

Paul's statement, "there is now no condemnation for those who are in Christ Jesus" (verse 1), refers back to his words in 5:12–21, where he demonstrated how those who belong to Jesus escape the condemnation that came to all people because of Adam's sin. The Holy Spirit exerts a liberating power through the work of Christ that takes those who belong to him out of the realm of sin and spiritual death. Paul reiterates this freedom was not achieved by the Mosaic law, which was powerless to save because it was "weakened by the flesh," but by the redemptive work of Jesus, who "condemned sin in the flesh" (verse 3).

Paul is careful to note that Jesus came in the *likeness* of sinful flesh to offer himself as a sacrifice for our sins. Jesus did indeed become fully human by taking on "flesh," but he did not—like every other person since Adam—succumb to the tyranny of the flesh. Rather, he became *like* us (in human flesh) so that we could become like him. Jesus condemned sin in the flesh so "that the righteous requirement of the law might be fully met in us" (verse 4). God, through Christ, has fulfilled the *entirety* of the law's demand on our behalf.

Paul concludes by presenting a series of contrasts between the flesh and the Spirit (see verses 5–8). His intention is to show that the *flesh* (the sinful nature) leads to death, while the *Spirit* (the godly nature) leads to life and peace. Those who are truly "in the realm of the Spirit" (verse 9) are assured of their future resurrection. Our part to play in this is to "put to death the misdeeds of the body" (verse 13). We must put into effect the new life God gives us. However, this response is itself empowered by the Spirit. We cannot stop committing sins in our own power; it can be done only by the power of the Holy Spirit at work in our lives.

❖ What contrasts does Paul draw between a mind that is fixed on the flesh and a mind that is focused on the things of the Holy Spirit?

Past to Present

Consider what this passage meant to the original readers and how it applies to us today.

Forming Your Mind

If you want to be healthy physically, you have to eat the right foods and engage in physical exercise. The same applies if you want to be healthy spiritually. If you are serious about becoming more like Christ, you have to "feed" your mind with spiritual food and engage in practices that lead you in that direction. It is by engaging with God's Word daily and spending time in his presence that you learn what the Spirit desires.

This raises an important question. *How are you forming your mind?* If you do not develop a practice of engaging with God and with Scripture, it is like having a diet that consists of unhealthy foods and never exercising. You can't expect such a lifestyle to yield good physical health. In the same way, you can't expect a lifestyle in which you never meditate on the things of God to yield good spiritual results.

❖ What does your "diet" consist of when it comes to your mind?

_____

_____

_____

_____

❖ What is one way you have learned to engage your mind in the things of the Spirit? How has that led to noticeable growth in your becoming more like Christ?

_____

_____

_____

_____

Committing to a Spiritual Life

Each year, high schoolers try out for band and are given a part to play. They have secured a spot for the season, but from there, their *success* depends on their actions. Some students, now that the audition is over, will be less dedicated in practicing. Other students, however, will redouble their efforts in practicing so they can improve over the season. Now, of those two groups, which do you think the band directors will focus more of their time and energy on helping? Most likely it will be the students who show dedication and the desire to improve.

Paul states the Holy Spirit's presence in your life will produce fruit that is pleasing to God. You are secure in him. However, the Spirit will not do his work apart from your response. Paul writes, "By the *Spirit you* put to death the misdeeds of the body" (verse 13, emphasis added). You can put sin to death only through the *Spirit's* power, but at the same time, the responsibility to put sin to death is on *your* shoulders. The Holy Spirit, like a good band director, will empower you to be successful—but you have to put in the effort to lead a godly and righteous life.

❖ Consider the two types of band students. Which groups would you put yourself in when it comes to putting sin to death? Why?

_____

_____

_____

_____

❖ What is some of the "fruit" that you know the Holy Spirit has produced in you? How would you describe your part in that fruit being present in your life?

_____

_____

_____

_____

Present Suffering and Future Glory [Romans 8:18–30]

[18] I consider that our present sufferings are not worth comparing with the glory that will be revealed in us. [19] For the creation waits in eager expectation for the children of God to be revealed. [20] For the creation was subjected to frustration, not by its own choice, but by the will of the one who subjected it, in hope [21] that the creation itself will be liberated from its bondage to decay and brought into the freedom and glory of the children of God.

[22] We know that the whole creation has been groaning as in the pains of childbirth right up to the present time. [23] Not only so, but we ourselves, who have the firstfruits of the Spirit, groan inwardly as we wait eagerly for our adoption to sonship, the redemption of our bodies. [24] For in this hope we were saved. But hope that is seen is no hope at all. Who hopes for what they already have? [25] But if we hope for what we do not yet have, we wait for it patiently.

[26] In the same way, the Spirit helps us in our weakness. We do not know what we ought to pray for, but the Spirit himself intercedes for us through wordless groans. [27] And he who searches our hearts knows the mind of the Spirit, because the Spirit intercedes for God's people in accordance with the will of God.

[28] And we know that in all things God works for the good of those who love him, who have been called according to his purpose. [29] For those God foreknew he also predestined to be conformed to the image of his Son, that he might be the firstborn among many brothers and sisters. [30] And those he predestined, he also called; those he called, he also justified; those he justified, he also glorified.

Original Meaning

Paul now highlights the future glory that awaits those who belong to Christ and walk according to the Spirit. He does not hide the fact that we *will* suffer on this earth but says this suffering will be *incomparable* to the glory that will one day be revealed in us (see verse 18). This future glory encompasses not only believers but also all of creation.

Following the lead of the psalmists, Paul personifies creation, using poetic language to speak of its "frustration" and eventual liberation (see verses 20–21). We likewise "groan inwardly" and yearn for the redemption of our physical bodies and our "adoption to sonship" (verse 23). This hope, anchored in God's promises, sustains us during trials and enables us to persevere.

Further, we have the assurance that God will provide the help we need to endure the tension between our present sufferings and future glory. The Holy Spirit "helps us in our weakness" (verse 26) and even intercedes for us when we do not know what to pray. These "wordless groans" of the Spirit align perfectly with God's will, ensuring the prayers we speak or even feel in our weakness are effective. The promise Paul expresses in verse 28 is one of the great biblical descriptions of providence. God, through his Spirit, causes "all things" to work for the good of "those who love him" and have been "called according to his purpose." This promise includes *all* aspects of our lives, even those moments of pain or confusion, because God sovereignly orchestrates everything for the ultimate good of his people.

Paul concludes by stating that God instituted a series of actions to create, sustain, and bring us to glory. God's first action was in "foreknowing" us, which in the biblical sense means that he entered into a relationship with us. This, in turn, led to God's decision to "predestine" us, which simply means he directed us to a particular goal: "to be conformed to the image of his Son, that he might be the firstborn among many brothers and sisters" (verse 29). Paul adds that those whom God predestines he also calls, justifies, and glorifies, which signifies the certainty of his plan. Note that even though our glorification is a future event, Paul uses the past tense ("glorified") to emphasize its assured fulfillment in God's eyes.

❖ How does Paul describe the sufferings you endure in this world? What help do you receive from the Holy Spirit when you are going through times of weakness and trial?

_____

_____

_____

_____

_____

_____

_____

_____

Past to Present

The Holy Spirit's Intercession

The book of Exodus relates an interesting interaction between God and Moses at the burning bush. The Lord instructed Moses to go to the Israelites and tell them of his plans to deliver them from bondage. But Moses had his doubts. One of his concerns was that he was not eloquent or quick when it came to speaking. God's response was that Moses was to go the people anyway and that he would give him the words to say (see Exodus 3:7–10; 4:10–12).

You might have the same kind of doubts that Moses had when it comes to your prayers. The situations you face are weighty and important. What if you pray the wrong thing? What if you forget something? What if your prayers don't get answered because you didn't exactly know *what* to pray? Paul's response to all these concerns is that "the Spirit himself intercedes for us" (Romans 8:26). The Holy Spirit steps in to help when you do not know what to pray—and his prayers are always right in line with God's will! So, just as Moses discovered, you don't have to be eloquent or quick with your speech. The Holy Spirit intercedes on your behalf.

❖ In what ways can you relate to Moses' concerns when God gave him a mission? When is a time you reacted to God in the same way?

_____

_____

_____

_____

❖ What are some of your doubts and fears involving prayer? How does it help you to know that the Holy Spirit intercedes for you when you don't know what to pray?

_____

_____

_____

_____

The Ultimate Good

Paul offers an interesting perspective when he writes, "We know that in all things God works for the good of those who love him" (verse 28). But what exactly does he mean? Is God like a cook who mixes all the "salty" and "sweet" ingredients of your life together to create a good dish? Or is God maybe like a coach who tells you to press through the pain you're enduring in the moment because it will lead to something "really good" for you down the road?

It is comforting to think God is promising something good *in this life.* But the reality is that God uses trials and suffering to produce Christian character in us, conform us into the likeness of Christ, and prepare us for final glory. So the "good" that God has in mind may not have anything to do with this life at all. For instance, he may allow you to lose a high-paying job in order to take you out of a materialistic lifestyle that does not honor his priorities—and you might never find such a job again. While God might give you something better in this life after a time of trial, testing, or suffering, his ultimate aim is for your *eternal* good.

❖ When is a time that God brought something good out of a situation that seemed only bad at the time? What did you learn about yourself through that experience?

_____

_____

_____

_____

_____

❖ How do you respond to the idea that the "good" the Lord is doing in you might not relate to this life at all? Why is it better that his aim is for your *eternal* good?

_____

_____

_____

_____

_____

More Than Conquerors [Romans 8:31–39]

[31] What, then, shall we say in response to these things? If God is for us, who can be against us? [32] He who did not spare his own Son, but gave him up for us all—how will he not also, along with him, graciously give us all things? [33] Who will bring any charge against those whom God has chosen? It is God who justifies. [34] Who then is the one who condemns? No one. Christ Jesus who died—more than that, who was raised to life—is at the right hand of God and is also interceding for us. [35] Who shall separate us from the love of Christ? Shall trouble or hardship or persecution or famine or nakedness or danger or sword? [36] As it is written:

"For your sake we face death all day long;
    we are considered as sheep to be slaughtered."

[37] No, in all these things we are more than conquerors through him who loved us. [38] For I am convinced that neither death nor life, neither angels nor demons, neither the present nor the future, nor any powers, [39] neither height nor depth, nor anything else in all creation, will be able to separate us from the love of God that is in Christ Jesus our Lord.

Original Meaning

Paul launches in a new direction with the question, "What, then, shall we say in response to these things?" (verse 31), with "these things" referring to the reasons for our confidence in Christ that he has outlined in chapters 5–8. Paul emphatically proclaims that God is "for us," as seen climactically in the giving of his beloved Son. If God has done that, we can be certain he will give us "all things" (verse 32) and that nothing can ultimately oppose us. No one can condemn us, because Jesus has died for us and been raised to life to be our intercessor.

Paul, borrowing from courtroom imagery, offers the assurance that every charge brought against us—whether by Satan or life's challenges—is unable to condemn us. Jesus not only defends us but also loves us and enters into relationship with us . . . and nothing will ever separate us from that love (see verses 33–35). Even though believers in Christ may face hardship, persecution, hunger, and danger (as Paul himself faced), none of these tribulations can ever jeopardize the bond between believers and Christ. The same God who delivered Paul from various trials (see 2 Corinthians 11:26–27; 12:10) is watching over each of us.

Paul concludes by stating that in all the varied difficulties of life, we are "more than conquerors" (Romans 8:37). He then offers his own personal testimony: "I am convinced . . ." (verse 38). Paul claims that *nothing* in all of creation—whether that involves death or life, things in the present or in the future, or things that come from above or below—can ever separate him from the "love of God that is in Christ Jesus our Lord" (verse 39). As Paul's chapter began with "no condemnation," so he now ends it with the bookend of "no separation."

❖ What evidence does Paul provide as to why God is "for us" (verse 31)? How does Paul answer his own question about who can condemn a follower of Christ?

_____

_____

_____

_____

_____

Past to Present

No Condemnation

Picture for a moment a courtroom scene. The judge sits at his bench up front ready to hear the case. The court reporter sits nearby waiting to document the proceedings. The bailiff stands at attention off to the side. The defense lawyer is stationed a ways back. On the opposite side is the prosecutor. He stands to his feet, points to the witness, and gets ready to make a charge. But before he can get the first word out, the judge interrupts him by slamming down the gavel. The judge then declares that *no condemnation* can come against the defendant.

This is the kind of scene that Paul depicts in this section of Romans. The enemy would like nothing more than to accuse and condemn you for violating God's holy law. He knows—and *you* know—that you are guilty of the charge. However, he is unable to bring any accusations against you, because you belong to Christ. God, the heavenly judge, has declared the penalty you rightly deserve to pay for breaking his law has already been paid through the sacrifice of his Son. The enemy thus has no standing. If you truly believe and embrace this, you can take a deep breath and let out a sigh of relief. For if *God* does not condemn you . . . no one will.

❖ What are some of the charges that the enemy has tried to make against you? What does Satan do to try and make you feel guilty for those things?

_____

_____

_____

_____

_____

❖ If you are in Christ, how have you sensed the Lord reassuring you that the enemy cannot bring any of these charges against you?

_____

_____

_____

_____

_____

No Separation

Go back to the courtroom scene and fix that image again in your mind. What happens when a defendant *is* found guilty of committing a crime? Well, if you have ever witnessed a courtroom proceeding, you know the next step after a verdict has been reached is for the judge to declare sentencing will be made. The judge may pass that sentence immediately or defer it to a later date. In many cases, the sentencing will include jail time or prison time for the defendant.

The idea behind sending a convicted person to jail or prison is to *separate* that individual from society. This is what the enemy of your soul would like to do in your case. He prowls around "like a roaring lion" (1 Peter 5:8) and tries to drive a wedge between you and God. Yet Paul's emphatic assertion is that neither Satan nor any other demonic powers can separate you "from the love of God that is in Christ Jesus" (Romans 8:39). If you belong to Christ and have accepted his sacrifice for your sin, you will never be condemned by the enemy. This means you will never be sentenced to separation from your heavenly Father.

❖ What are some ways that come to mind of how Satan and his demonic forces have tried to drive a wedge between you and God?

_____

_____

_____

_____

_____

❖ How does it reassure you to know that Satan—nor anything else— can never separate you from God's love? How can that help you to fight back against the enemy?

_____

_____

_____

_____

_____

Closing Prayer: Lord God, I entrust my life to you and submit myself to your will. I proclaim here and now that Jesus has destroyed the power of condemnation and that the enemy can make no claim against me. I now stand before you, Father, dressed in your righteousness. Remind me every day that I can never be separated from your presence, because I am your child. Amen.

8

It's All About God

Romans 9:1-13, 19-29; 9:30-10:13

Experts in child psychology tell us that human beings are born inherently self-centered. This is because babies must depend on their parents (or caregivers) for everything during their first years of life. They *have* to be egocentric to get their needs met—it's a vital aspect of their survival. So they cry, and complain, and throw temper tantrums, and do whatever else is necessary to get what they want . . . without ever giving a thought about how their actions are impacting others. They are unable to see the world any other way.

We expect babies and toddlers to behave in this self-centered manner. Yet there comes a time when we expect that most children will mature to the point where they *can* consider another person's point of view. Experts tell us this most often occurs when children reach the age of four or five. Around that stage, we want children to start learning how to share with others and begin to understand that not everything is always about them.

The Jewish people of Paul's day were under the mistaken belief it was *all about them*. They considered themselves to be saved simply because they were of Jewish descent. What Paul tells them in this next section of Romans—with "great sorrow and unceasing anguish" (9:2)—is that it is time for them to mature and realize it is *all about God* and his designs for humanity. The Lord has ordained that salvation comes through faith in Jesus alone, and those who refuse the salvation that God offers—whether Jew or Gentile—will face his judgment.

True Children of God [Romans 9:1-13]

[1] I speak the truth in Christ—I am not lying, my conscience confirms it through the Holy Spirit— [2] I have great sorrow and unceasing anguish in my heart. [3] For I could wish that I myself were cursed and cut off from Christ for the sake of my people, those of my own race, [4] the people of Israel. Theirs is the adoption to sonship; theirs the divine glory, the covenants, the receiving of the law, the temple worship and the promises. [5] Theirs are the patriarchs, and from them is traced the human ancestry of the Messiah, who is God over all, forever praised! Amen.

[6] It is not as though God's word had failed. For not all who are descended from Israel are Israel. [7] Nor because they are his descendants are they all Abraham's children. On the contrary, "It is through Isaac that your offspring will be reckoned." [8] In other words, it is not the children by physical descent who are God's children, but it is the children of the promise who are regarded as Abraham's offspring. [9] For this was how the promise was stated: "At the appointed time I will return, and Sarah will have a son."

[10] Not only that, but Rebekah's children were conceived at the same time by our father Isaac. [11] Yet, before the twins were born or had done anything good or bad—in order that God's purpose in election might stand: [12] not by works but by him who calls—she was told, "The older will serve the younger." [13] Just as it is written: "Jacob I loved, but Esau I hated."

Original Meaning

After Paul's celebration of God's faithfulness to us in Christ, we would expect him to spell out the implications of that theology for Christian living. Instead, he launches into a discussion of Israel's response to the gospel. Why tackle *that* topic? One reason is certainly because Paul's aim in Romans has been to show the gospel is the good news sent by the *God of the Old Testament*. For Paul, there can be no good news in Christ unless what God did through him was part of the master plan as revealed in the Old Testament.

Paul feels "unceasing anguish" (verse 2) when he considers the state of his people. God had given them so much—adoption as his people, his glory, the covenants, the law, temple worship, his promises, and the patriarchs (see verses 4–5)—and yet because they had rejected the Messiah, they were not saved. This is not because "God's word had failed" (verse 6). The fact that the majority of Jews rejected Jesus cannot lead to the conclusion that God's plans and promises had gone awry. For if God had gone back on his word to Israel, it means a chasm exists between the Old and New Testaments, and the plan of salvation crashes.

Rather, Paul argues that "not all who are descended from Israel are Israel" (verse 6). God has always chosen some from within national Israel to be his people (what the prophets called a "remnant") and reserved the right to determine who his people would be. So there is, in a sense, both a *physical* Israel and a *spiritual* Israel. In Galatians 6:16, Paul refers to the church as "Israel," so it is likely this is what he has in mind when he refers to a spiritual Israel. Jews belong to physical Israel by birth, but only those who accept Jesus as the Messiah belong to the spiritual Israel. The Bible thus does not teach that all people of Jewish descent are automatically saved. Instead, it teaches that all people— Jewish and Gentile—need to be saved.

❖ What evidence does Paul us to support his argument, "Not all who are descended from [physical] Israel are [spiritual] Israel" (verse 6)?

_____

_____

_____

_____

Past to Present

Consider what this passage meant to the original readers and how it applies to us today.

Count Your Blessings

You've heard the idiom "count your blessings." There are many reasons why this is a good idea, but one in particular is that it helps you not take your blessings for granted. The Israelites had received many blessings from God. They were witnesses to his divine glory. They were the only people on earth who received his instructions on how to live through the law. They received the benefit of the covenants that God made between himself and people like Abraham, Moses, and David. They received "adoption" as a national blessing. God chose them "out of all the peoples on the face of the earth to be his people" (Deuteronomy 7:6).

Sadly, many of the Jews had misinterpreted these blessings and promises from God as a guarantee of their eternal security. They had failed to realize it is not "children by physical descent" but "children of the promise" who are saved (Romans 9:8). In the same way, we must never take for granted the blessings that God has given us in Christ. The fact that God has saved us should never lull us into the complacency of thinking we have "arrived" in our spiritual journey. Rather, the knowledge that we have been saved from our sin should compel us to seek a God-honoring life and share the message of the gospel with the world.

❖ What are some of the blessings God has provided to you that you might be overlooking in your life right now? Why do you think it is often so easy to take God's blessings for granted?

❖ What is the danger in thinking you have "arrived" when it comes to your faith? What steps are you taking to actively grow in your faith?

_____

_____

_____

_____

Connect the Dots

Have you ever done a connect-the-dots puzzle? You start with a page filled with little dots and numbers. By drawing a line between one dot to the next, a picture begins to emerge. You can't see the picture until you actually go through the effort of connecting the dots. Paul is "connecting the dots" for his readers in this portion of Romans to reveal the "big picture" of God's plan. By his day, it was evident most Jews had not responded to gospel. But the response among the Gentiles had been different. They were hungry, open, and responsive.

The situation caused some to wonder if "God's word had failed" (verse 6). Had God given up on his promises to Israel and turned his back on them? The answer from Paul is _no_. God is sovereign and acts according to his purposes—and his purposes alone. We often won't know what God's plans are or how he is at work, but we can trust that he never goes back on his word or fails to deliver on his promises. Even when we can't see what the big picture is behind the dots on the page, we can trust that God does and will never fail us.

❖ Why is it important for you personally to see the connection between the Old and New Testaments when it comes to the overall plan of God's salvation?

_____

_____

_____

_____

❖ What are some of the ways that God has helped you connect the dots in your life when it comes to understanding his truths?

_____

_____

_____

_____

God Is Sovereign [Romans 9:19–29]

[19] One of you will say to me: "Then why does God still blame us? For who is able to resist his will?" [20] But who are you, a human being, to talk back to God? "Shall what is formed say to the one who formed it, 'Why did you make me like this?'" [21] Does not the potter have the right to make out of the same lump of clay some pottery for special purposes and some for common use?

[22] What if God, although choosing to show his wrath and make his power known, bore with great patience the objects of his wrath— prepared for destruction? [23] What if he did this to make the riches of his glory known to the objects of his mercy, whom he prepared in advance for glory— [24] even us, whom he also called, not only from the Jews but also from the Gentiles? [25] As he says in Hosea:

"I will call them 'my people' who are not my people;
and I will call her 'my loved one' who is not my loved one,"

[26] and,

"In the very place where it was said to them,
'You are not my people,'
there they will be called 'children of the living God.'"

[27] Isaiah cries out concerning Israel:

"Though the number of the Israelites be like the sand by the sea,
only the remnant will be saved.

²⁸ For the Lord will carry out
   his sentence on earth with speed and finality."

²⁹ It is just as Isaiah said previously:

"Unless the Lord Almighty
   had left us descendants,
we would have become like Sodom,
   we would have been like Gomorrah."

Original Meaning

Paul's discussion of God's sovereignty in choosing his people prompts him to engage in another round of questions and answers with a fictional sparring partner. Paul's first perceived objection is how God can hold humanity accountable if no one can resist his will (see verse 19). His answer is simply that God holds all authority and we have neither the means nor right to question his purposes. Just as a potter has the right to make anything out of a lump of clay (an image rooted in the Old Testament), so God has the right to extend mercy or judgment as he desires.

Continuing the discourse, Paul asks a series of questions to elaborate on God's patience with sinners (see verses 22–24). Behind this section is a Jewish tradition that questioned why God was waiting so long to judge sinners and establish justice in the world. Paul addresses the issue by stating God is using this time before the end to prepare for an even greater display of his powerful judgment and to bring glory to his chosen people. This contrast between wrath and glory shows that Paul is writing about individuals destined for judgment on the one hand and individuals destined for glory on the other. *Salvation* is the issue.

Paul concludes his argument by focusing on the inclusion of Gentiles in God's plan (see verses 24–29). He draws on Hosea to show how they have been transferred from the status of "not my people" and "not my loved one" to the status of "my people," "my loved one," and "children of the living God." Under the new covenant, God shows no distinction between Jew and Gentile but offers grace to each alike. The passages from Isaiah emphasize that God will save a remnant from Israel. They offer hope to Israel, for God is determined to persevere "descendants" for Israel—people who will inherit his promise to Abraham.

❖ What are some of the reasons for why God is patient with sinners?

_____

_____

_____

_____

Past to Present

Respecting God's Authority

Imagine a newly enlisted soldier in basic training. He has been in the military for precisely three days and has not slept well any of those nights. The problem, he determines, is his bunk bed. So he seeks out the company commander on base. "Sir," he says, "you need to look into the beds in the barracks. If you want some suggestions, let me know."

Of course, newly enlisted soldiers would never do this because they know that privates don't make demands on higher-ranking officers. Yet this is often what we do with God! We see things from our vantage point, determine it's not working for us, and complain about it. While Jesus said our heavenly Father gives "good gifts to those who ask him" (Matthew 7:11), we don't have the right to *demand* those gifts from him.

❖ Do you tend to demand things from God? If so, what would be a better way to present your requests to him?

_____

_____

_____

_____

❖ Do you tend to believe that you know what "good gifts" the Lord should be providing? What is the danger in believing you know better than God what is best for you?

_____

_____

_____

_____

Modeling God's Patience

A Jewish tradition existed in Paul's day that questioned why God was waiting so long to judge sinners and establish justice on earth. The cry of the martyrs in Revelation 6:10 reflects this basic question: "How long, Sovereign Lord, holy and true, until you judge the inhabitants of the earth and avenge our blood?" Paul's answer is that God is being patient with sinners so he can ultimately display his wrath and power more clearly and bring glory to his chosen people. God's mercy will one day end, but in the meantime he is being patient.

This should raise some important questions if you are a follower of Christ. Are you being patient with others in the same way God is being patient with them? Are you willing to forgive others when they commit wrongs against you? Or are you rushing to make judgments against them and cutting them out of your life? Paul wrote in Ephesians that you are to forgive others "just as in Christ God forgave you" (4:32). God has forgiven you greatly and has demonstrated his patience toward you. Are you extending that same courtesy to others?

❖ Why does God ask you to be patient with others? What are some ways recently you have forgiven others just as God has forgiven you?

_____

_____

_____

_____

❖ How does it encourage you to know that God *will* one day execute his judgment against evil? Why is it important for all followers of Jesus to understand this reality?

_____

_____

_____

_____

The Bottom Line [Romans 9:30–10:13]

9:30 What then shall we say? That the Gentiles, who did not pursue righteousness, have obtained it, a righteousness that is by faith; 31 but the people of Israel, who pursued the law as the way of righteousness, have not attained their goal. 32 Why not? Because they pursued it not by faith but as if it were by works. They stumbled over the stumbling stone. 33 As it is written:

> "See, I lay in Zion a stone that causes people to stumble
>> and a rock that makes them fall,
>> and the one who believes in him will never be put to shame."

10:1 Brothers and sisters, my heart's desire and prayer to God for the Israelites is that they may be saved. 2 For I can testify about them that they are zealous for God, but their zeal is not based on knowledge. 3 Since they did not know the righteousness of God and sought to establish their own, they did not submit to God's righteousness. 4 Christ is the culmination of the law so that there may be righteousness for everyone who believes.

5 Moses writes this about the righteousness that is by the law: "The person who does these things will live by them." 6 But the righteousness that is by faith says: "Do not say in your heart, 'Who will ascend into heaven?'" (that is, to bring Christ down) 7 "or 'Who will descend into the deep?'" (that is, to bring Christ up from the dead). 8 But what does it say? "The word is near you; it is in your mouth and in your heart," that is, the

message concerning faith that we proclaim: ⁹ If you declare with your mouth, "Jesus is Lord," and believe in your heart that God raised him from the dead, you will be saved. ¹⁰ For it is with your heart that you believe and are justified, and it is with your mouth that you profess your faith and are saved. ¹¹ As Scripture says, "Anyone who believes in him will never be put to shame." ¹² For there is no difference between Jew and Gentile—the same Lord is Lord of all and richly blesses all who call on him, ¹³ for, "Everyone who calls on the name of the Lord will be saved."

Original Meaning

Paul's statement, "What then shall we say?" (9:30), indicates he is shifting focus. In this section, he will explore themes of righteousness and faith while explaining Israel's failure to embrace the blessings of salvation found in Christ. Two forms of righteousness are contrasted: *righteousness through faith* and *righteousness through the law*. The Gentiles, who were not pursuing righteousness, attained it through faith, while the Jews, who were pursuing righteousness by the law, failed to achieve it because they sought it through works (see verses 30–32). This distinction reflects a central problem in Israel—misplacing focus on the law's works while failing to recognize faith in Christ as the culmination of God's redemptive plan. Jesus is the "stone" over which Israel has stumbled.

Paul makes it clear how deeply he feels about the failure of Israel to embrace the salvation that God offers in Jesus (see 10:1–4). He regards the zeal of his fellow Israelites as a good thing. The problem is that—like the pre-Christian Paul—their zeal is not directed by knowledge. They do not understand that God is now offering a right relationship with himself through faith in Christ, the culmination of salvation history. In seeking to establish their own righteousness, they are also guilty of relying on their own works.

Paul concludes by quoting Leviticus 18:5 and Deuteronomy 30:10–14 to emphasize the difference between law-based righteousness and faith-based righteousness. Through Jesus' incarnation and resurrection, righteousness has been made available to all. It only requires belief in the heart and confession with the mouth that "Jesus is Lord" (Romans 10:9). Paul cites Joel 2:32 to reiterate that "everyone who calls on the name of the Lord will be saved" (verse 13). As a result of Jesus' coming and bringing the law to its culmination, righteousness is now available for all who believe. Faith, apart from ethnic origin or works, is the sole basis for experiencing this gift that Christ offers to the world.

❖ What does Paul say about the Israelites' zeal? In what way are the people of Israel demonstrating that their zeal is misplaced?

Past to Present

Isn't It Ironic?

Something is considered *ironic* when it leads to an outcome opposite of the one expected. A fire station burning to the ground is ironic because fire stations are supposed to fight fires. A professional chef burning her dinner is ironic because chefs are expected to be skilled in cooking. A traffic officer getting a speeding ticket is ironic because officers are supposed to enforce traffic laws. According to Paul, the Gentiles receiving righteousness as a result of their faith in Jesus is also ironic. It is unexpected for this group, who did not have the benefit of receiving God's laws like the Israelites, to be the ones to receive salvation.

This only goes to show that God often works in ways we do not expect. For this reason, we can never count anyone out of God's plan of salvation. If the Gentiles of Paul's day—who came from backgrounds involving the worship of pagan gods—could accept the gospel and turn from their unrighteousness, so God can transform any person today through the gospel and set him or her on the path of righteousness. Our part is to never give up on *anyone*. We might consider certain people in our lives to be "too far gone" for the gospel to make an impact on them. But God never gives up on anyone and is always seeking to bring the lost into his family.

❖ What are some of the things in your life (or the life of a loved one) that God accomplished in ways you didn't expect?

_____

_____

_____

_____

❖ Who is someone you might unconsciously be "giving up on" when it comes to salvation? What needs to specifically change in your attitude toward that person?

_____

_____

_____

_____

The Unfinished Task

We all have tasks on our to-do lists that are unfinished. For the most part, the delay causes no harm. It's no big deal if we wait a week to wash the car. No huge issues will arise if we can't get to mowing the lawn on the day we had planned. Mopping the floor? It can wait another day. Yet the same cannot be said of our "to-do" list item of sharing the gospel. This task, assigned by Jesus himself, might just be the most important responsibility bestowed on us.

When Paul writes that his "heart's desire and prayer to God for the Israelites is that they may be saved" (10:1), he is expressing the deep commitment he feels for sharing the gospel to all—Jews and Gentiles alike. Proclaiming the message of the gospel to the nations is the great-and-yet-unfinished task for all followers of Christ. For this reason, we need to stay focused on that goal. Our heart's desire, like Paul's, must be to save everyone we can from God's judgment.

❖ What are the recurring distractions in your life that get in the way of you sharing your faith with others? What is necessary for you to remove those distractions?

_____

_____

_____

_____

_____

❖ What are some of the best ways you have found to naturally share the grace and truth of Jesus with the people you love who are not yet following him?

_____

_____

_____

_____

_____

Closing Prayer: Jesus, thank you for bestowing your righteousness on me. I believe in my heart and confess with my mouth that you are Lord! Help me to remember you are the potter and I am the clay. I don't want to spend my life questioning your plans—I want to invest my life in leaning into your plans and telling others about you. Thank you for empowering me to share this good news with ever-increasing passion, confidence, and impact. For your glory. Amen.

9

God's Chosen People

Romans 10:14–11:6; 11:11–24, 25–36

We live in a world where people can be "canceled" if their words or deeds are deemed objectionable. The phenomenon most frequently occurs with public figures who, in some way, were previously *chosen* and *accepted* by society. The cancellation might take the form of boycotts, social media ostracization, and calls for the person's removal from influence. But whatever form it takes, the goal is to let the world know the once-accepted person has now been rejected by the culture at large.

Paul has just argued in Romans that "it is not the children by physical descent who are God's children, but it is the children of the promise who are regarded as Abraham's offspring" (9:8). God, in his mercy, has determined that all who put their faith in Christ will be saved and treated as members of his own family. Yet this raises questions about God's original chosen people—the Jewish race. Are they now canceled in God's sight because of their refusal to accept Jesus as their Messiah? Have they forfeited their claims to the promises God made to them? In Paul's own words, "Did they stumble so as to fall beyond recovery?"

The apostle's answer to these questions is, "Not at all!" (11:11). He goes on to explain, "Israel has experienced a hardening in part until the full number of the Gentiles has come in, and in this way all Israel will be saved" (verse 25–26). There has been great debate for centuries about how this will happen . . . and we won't settle the matter in this lesson.

But what we can say is that God's patience for stubborn people is vast and his mercy is great. He loves *every* nation and people group—including the Jewish people—and his grace is big enough for us all.

Faith Comes by Hearing [Romans 10:14–11:6]

10:14 How, then, can they call on the one they have not believed in? And how can they believe in the one of whom they have not heard? And how can they hear without someone preaching to them? 15 And how can anyone preach unless they are sent? As it is written: "How beautiful are the feet of those who bring good news!"

16 But not all the Israelites accepted the good news. For Isaiah says, "Lord, who has believed our message?" 17 Consequently, faith comes from hearing the message, and the message is heard through the word about Christ. 18 But I ask: Did they not hear? Of course they did:

"Their voice has gone out into all the earth,
their words to the ends of the world."

19 Again I ask: Did Israel not understand? First, Moses says,

"I will make you envious by those who are not a nation;
I will make you angry by a nation that has no understanding."

20 And Isaiah boldly says,

"I was found by those who did not seek me;
I revealed myself to those who did not ask for me."

21 But concerning Israel he says,

"All day long I have held out my hands
to a disobedient and obstinate people."

11:1 I ask then: Did God reject his people? By no means! I am an Israelite myself, a descendant of Abraham, from the tribe of Benjamin. 2 God did not reject his people, whom he foreknew. Don't you know what Scripture says in the passage about Elijah—how he appealed to God against Israel: ³ "Lord, they have killed your prophets and torn down your altars; I am the only one left, and they are trying to kill me"? ⁴ And what was God's answer to him? "I have reserved for myself seven thousand who have not bowed the knee to Baal." ⁵ So too, at the present time there is a remnant chosen by grace. ⁶ And if by grace, then it cannot be based on works; if it were, grace would no longer be grace.

Original Meaning

Paul's discussion in this section again revolves around salvation, particularly as it relates to both Jews and Gentiles. Paul begins by drawing on the prophecy of Joel 2:32, which promises salvation to "everyone who calls on the name of the LORD," to outline the steps necessary for salvation: the sending of preachers, preaching, hearing the message about Jesus, believing in Christ, and calling on the name of the Lord (see Romans 10:14–15). Paul quotes from Isaiah 52:7 to assert the necessity of proclaiming the gospel—noting that preachers have indeed been sent to proclaim the "good news," ensuring that people *can* hear and believe.

However, Israel—in spite of having heard the gospel (see verse 18) and having understood its implications (see verse 19)—has remained largely unresponsive. Paul draws on Isaiah 53:1 (verse 16) and Deuteronomy 32:21 (verse 19) to illustrate how Israel had a history of rejecting the good news of God. This rejection is contrasted with the Gentiles who, though not actively seeking God (see verse 20), have found him and embraced the righteousness that comes through faith. The vivid picture that Paul paints is one of the Gentiles receiving grace while Israel stands resistant in spite of God's continuous outreach to them.

Paul concludes by asking, "Did God reject his people?" His answer is, "By no means!" (11:1). God did *not* reject his people, whom he "foreknew" or chose ahead of time (verse 2). Paul has *physical* Israel in view here and is affirming that God chose Israel as his own people. However, from that group he chose a "remnant," as revealed by God to Elijah (see verses 2–4). Paul's conclusion is that "so too, at the present time there is a remnant chosen by grace" (verse 5). God's Word affirms a continuing role for Israel in salvation history. But Israel cannot claim this role as a matter of right, for it is due solely to the working of God's grace.

❖ What point is Paul making about Israel's opportunity to receive the gospel? What does he mean when he states that God has called out a "remnant" from among his people?

_____

_____

_____

_____

Past to Present

Consider what this passage meant to the original readers and how it applies to us today.

Preaching the Gospel

Paul opens this section of Romans with an explanation of how people come to faith in Christ. He states first that people cannot "call on" Jesus if they have not "believed in" him. This can't happen if they "have not heard" about Christ. For them to hear, there must be someone who is there to "[preach] to them" (10:14). And for that to happen, there must be people in the church who are willing to go or be "sent" to bring the gospel to those who need to receive it.

In Paul's day, before the New Testament was written, the way everyone heard about the gospel was through ambassadors (such as himself) preaching the gospel. Today, we might assume that since the Bible is so widely available, people can just read about salvation and come to faith in Jesus by themselves. Yet the research consistently shows that the majority of people accept Christ through the influence of *others*—especially family and friends. Each of us still has a part to play in preaching the gospel! We are *all* ambassadors for Christ.

❖ How do you respond to Paul's presentation of how the gospel comes to people? What role does "preaching the gospel" serve today?

_____

_____

_____

_____

❖ What are some of the ways you are preaching the gospel—whether that is through the words you say or the way you lead your life?

_____

_____

_____

_____

Hearing the Gospel

Paul does not deny the Israelites were God's chosen people. They had even received the special privilege of being among the first to hear the good news when Jesus proclaimed that God's kingdom had arrived on earth. The people of Israel had *heard* and been given the opportunity to *understand* this message. Some, like the twelve disciples and faithful followers of Jesus, had *accepted* the good news. But there were many among Israel who refused to hear.

When Jesus taught, he would often say, "Whoever has ears, let them hear" (Matthew 11:15). The implication is that not everyone had spiritual "ears" to hear the truths he was offering. Sadly, the same happens in churches today. We, much like the Israelites in Paul's day, have the opportunity to *hear* and *understand* the deep truths of God. But so often we, also like the Israelites, feel we have some special privilege with God due to our regular church attendance, baptism, giving, acts of service, and the like. God is calling us to go deeper with him. The question is whether we will respond to that call with "ears to hear."

❖ How would you describe the difference between *hearing* the gospel and *responding* to it?

_____

_____

_____

_____

❖ What steps are you taking to understand the deeper truths of God? What steps do you feel you *need* to take in this regard?

_____

_____

_____

_____

Ingrafted Branches [Romans 11:11–24]

¹¹ Again I ask: Did they stumble so as to fall beyond recovery? Not at all! Rather, because of their transgression, salvation has come to the Gentiles to make Israel envious. ¹² But if their transgression means riches for the world, and their loss means riches for the Gentiles, how much greater riches will their full inclusion bring!

¹³ I am talking to you Gentiles. Inasmuch as I am the apostle to the Gentiles, I take pride in my ministry ¹⁴ in the hope that I may somehow arouse my own people to envy and save some of them. ¹⁵ For if their rejection brought reconciliation to the world, what will their acceptance be but life from the dead? ¹⁶ If the part of the dough offered as firstfruits is holy, then the whole batch is holy; if the root is holy, so are the branches.

¹⁷ If some of the branches have been broken off, and you, though a wild olive shoot, have been grafted in among the others and now share in the nourishing sap from the olive root, ¹⁸ do not consider yourself to be superior to those other branches. If you do, consider this: You do not support the root, but the root supports you. ¹⁹ You will say then, "Branches were broken off so that I could be grafted in." ²⁰ Granted. But they were broken off because of unbelief, and you stand by faith. Do not be arrogant, but tremble. ²¹ For if God did not spare the natural branches, he will not spare you either.

²² Consider therefore the kindness and sternness of God: sternness to those who fell, but kindness to you, provided that you continue in his kindness. Otherwise, you also will be cut off. ²³ And if they do not persist in unbelief, they will be grafted in, for God is able to graft them in again. ²⁴ After all, if you were cut out of an olive tree that is wild by nature, and contrary to nature were grafted into a cultivated olive tree, how much more readily will these, the natural branches, be grafted into their own olive tree!

Original Meaning

The preaching of the gospel had divided Israel into two groups: (1) a minority (the "remnant"), who had received salvation; and (2) the majority, whose hearts had been hardened. Paul now asks whether this situation is permanent. His answer? "Not at all!" (verse 11). Israel's rejection of God's grace in Christ had led to salvation for the Gentiles. God's *plan* for the salvation of the world included this Jewish rejection and Gentile acceptance—and the salvation of Gentiles served the purpose of making Israel "envious." Israel's loss meant "riches for the Gentiles" (verse 12), but greater riches will come with the "full inclusion" of the Jews. The blessing Israel will experience comes by way of an increase in the number of Jews who are saved.

Paul now turns to address any Gentile Christians who presume they have replaced Israel in God's plan. Paul states they are a "wild olive shoot" (verse 17) that has been grafted into the "natural branches" (verse 21) of Israel. The Gentiles received the blessings of Israel not by their merit but by faith and God's grace. It is through the "root," representing the Jewish patriarchs (Israel's foundational relationship with God), that the Gentiles have gained their inclusion. For this reason, they must not boast or be arrogant, for their continued faith is essential to maintaining their place within God's people (see verses 18–22). Paul's warning serves as both a theological reminder and a call for humility among the Gentile believers in Rome.

Paul concludes the analogy of the olive tree with a word of hope for the Jews. Just as the Gentile Christians run the risk of being "cut off" (verse 22) if they stop believing, so Jews can be "grafted in" (verse 23) if they turn from unbelief to faith in Christ. After all, it is easier to graft natural branches back in than to do what God has already done "contrary to nature" (verse 24)—grafting in the wild olive shoots. Paul stops short here of predicting that God will graft unbelieving Israel back into the people of God again . . . but only just short.

❖ What reasons does Paul give as to why the Gentile Christians should not boast or presume they have replaced Israel in God's plan?

_____

_____

_____

_____

Past to Present

Grafted into God's Family

Paul uses the analogy of an olive tree to show how the Gentiles have been "grafted" into God's plans. Grafting olive branches is a technique dating back thousands of years that allows for the combination of desirable traits from different trees. The process involves cutting a shoot from the desired olive variety, making a cleft in the rootstock (established tree), and then placing and aligning the shoot in the rootstock so the two will join together and grow.

The incredible news of the gospel is that God has invited *all* people to join his family. Just as a shoot is grafted into an established tree, so the Gentiles have been grafted into God's people of Israel. All that is required is faith in Jesus. So, the next time you wonder if the Lord has plans for you, remember this truth. God has chosen to bring you into what was once reserved for his chosen people. He bestows on you the same blessings he bestowed on them.

❖ How do you respond to the fact that you have been grafted into the family that God began with the Israelites? What kind of heritage does that mean you have?

_____

_____

_____

_____

❖ Do you ever wonder if God truly has plans for your life? What does the reality that God brought you into his own family reveal about his intentions toward you?

_____

_____

_____

_____

Pitfalls of Pride

Paul writes that he takes pride in being "the apostle to the Gentiles" (verse 13). While God's call to him included ministry to both Jews and Gentiles, he became God's point man in bringing the gospel to the Gentiles. Given this, it's easy to imagine Gentile Christians citing Paul's focus on them as evidence that God has turned his back on Israel. But Paul will not tolerate that kind of pride in people. Rather, he tells them, "Do not be arrogant, but tremble. For if God did not spare the natural branches, he will not spare you either" (verses 20–21).

We all must come to grips with the seriousness of this warning. It is only by God's grace that *any* of us—Jew or Gentile—are saved. As Paul wrote previously in Romans, "God does not show favoritism" (2:11). When we fall into the error of thinking we are somehow "special" or "more deserving" of God's mercy than others, we open ourselves to pride and complacency. Jesus' commission to his followers is to "make disciples of all nations" (Matthew 28:19). We need to focus our efforts on *reaching* the lost instead of feeling we are *superior* to them.

❖ What do you think it means to "tremble" when you consider what God has done for you?

_____

_____

_____

❖ What are some of the dangers of pride that you have seen when it comes to following after Jesus? Why does God stress that he doesn't show favoritism for any group of people?

_____

_____

_____

All Israel Will Be Saved [Romans 11:25–36]

25 I do not want you to be ignorant of this mystery, brothers and sisters, so that you may not be conceited: Israel has experienced a hardening in

part until the full number of the Gentiles has come in, [26] and in this way all Israel will be saved. As it is written:

"The deliverer will come from Zion;
   he will turn godlessness away from Jacob.
[27] And this is my covenant with them
   when I take away their sins."

[28] As far as the gospel is concerned, they are enemies for your sake; but as far as election is concerned, they are loved on account of the patriarchs, [29] for God's gifts and his call are irrevocable. [30] Just as you who were at one time disobedient to God have now received mercy as a result of their disobedience, [31] so they too have now become disobedient in order that they too may now receive mercy as a result of God's mercy to you. [32] For God has bound everyone over to disobedience so that he may have mercy on them all.

[33] Oh, the depth of the riches of the wisdom and knowledge of God!
   How unsearchable his judgments,
   and his paths beyond tracing out!
[34] "Who has known the mind of the Lord?
   Or who has been his counselor?"
[35] "Who has ever given to God,
   that God should repay them?"
[36] For from him and through him and for him are all things.
   To him be the glory forever! Amen.

Original Meaning

Paul previously stated if the Jews "do not persist in unbelief, they will be grafted in" (verse 23). He now reveals Israel's hardening is temporary, lasting until "the full number of the Gentiles has come in" (verse 25). If "all Israel" refers to a single generation, it likely represents Israel as it exists in the end times (the quotations Paul uses from Isaiah

59:20–21 and 27:9 point in this direction). Paul is thus predicting the salvation of a significant number of Jews at the time of Jesus' return. The present remnant of Israel will be expanded to include a larger number who will enter the eternal kingdom with converted Gentiles.

Paul provides further evidence in verses 28–32 that "all Israel will be saved" (verse 26) and highlights the interplay between Israel's disobedience and God's mercy. While Israel's rejection of the gospel made them "enemies" of God regarding salvation, they remain loved due to God's promises to the patriarchs. God's gifts and calling are irrevocable, ensuring Israel's continuing election. Paul emphasizes God's plan to extend mercy to Jews and Gentiles equally—Israel's disobedience has brought mercy to the Gentiles, which will, in turn, lead to Israel's inclusion. Ultimately, again, God's purpose is to demonstrate mercy to all.

Paul caps off his survey of salvation history by marveling at the depth of God's plan for humankind. He acknowledges that God's judgments and ways are "unsearchable" and "beyond tracing out" (verse 33). The rhetorical questions that follow in verses 34–35 are taken from the Old Testament (Isaiah 40:13 and likely Job 41:11) and emphasize that no one can comprehend God's mind or render him indebted to humanity. God does not do anything in his plan of salvation because anyone has earned his favor but solely because of his great love. Paul closes in verse 36 by reminding us that God is ultimate in all things and therefore is deserving of our praise.

❖ What is the "mystery" that Paul describes for his readers? What is his conclusion about God's plans for saving "all Israel" (verse 26)?

_____

_____

_____

_____

_____

Past to Present

Motivated by Love

We all like a good mystery . . . especially when it is solved. This section of Romans represents the "mystery" of God's plan for Israel—a truth hidden in the past but now disclosed in the gospel. The Old Testament predicted Gentiles would join Jews in worshiping the Lord in the last days. But wholly novel is the idea that the bulk of Israel will wait to enjoy the blessings of the kingdom until the set number of Gentiles has come in. What is clear is that God does not give up on Israel.

Love requires a choice. If a man gives a woman a ring and says, "Now you owe me your love," she will find it manipulative. He can't force her love. But if he give the ring and says, "I want to spend the rest of my life with you . . . will you marry me?" it has a whole different feel. A choice is now involved, and the woman can respond, "Yes, I love you too and want to marry you." In the same way, God offers us a choice. We can choose to accept or reject his love. But he will never force it on us.

❖ God's love is the motivator behind his plan of salvation. How does the life, death, and resurrection of Jesus reveal God's stunning and unmerited love toward you?

_____

_____

_____

_____

❖ What are some ways that God has shown his love to you? How did you recognize he was demonstrating his love to you?

_____

_____

_____

_____

Humbled Before God

Paul ends this section with a *doxology*. The word derives from the Latin terms *doxa*, meaning "opinion" or "glory," and *logia*, which refers to "oral or written expression." Paul's intent behind his doxology—his written expression of praise to God—is to motivate us to humbly consider God's extraordinary plan for the world. The key idea here is *humility*. Not only are we to put aside any pride when considering what the Lord has done for us but we should also adopt an attitude of awe at what he has done.

Jesus said, "Seek first [God's] kingdom and his righteousness" (Matthew 6:33). Putting the Lord's agenda first means putting ours second. It means submitting our will to his and allowing his kingdom priorities to rule our lives. Humility is the appropriate attitude for us finite creatures as we seek to plumb the depths of God's character and truth.

❖ Why is humility the proper posture for a Christian? What message do you send to God when you demonstrate a lack of humility?

❖ How is authentic humility a witness to other believers? How can it become a testimony to those who are not yet followers of Jesus?

Closing Prayer: God of love, through the centuries your people have rebelled, resisted, and run from you. Thank you for never giving up on us. Thank you for your plan of salvation, your enduring patience, and your endless love toward me. Thank you for choosing me to be among your people. Amen.

10

Sacrificial Living

Romans 12:1-8, 9-21; 13:8-14

What comes to mind when you hear the word *sacrifice*? Perhaps you picture the Jewish priests in Old Testament times who offered up animal sacrifices to the Lord in the temple. Or maybe the image that jumps into your head is more along the lines of giving up something you value for another. Or perhaps your idea of sacrifice is regularly giving your time or money to support a ministry in your church.

In each of these cases, the sacrifice comes with a *cost*. In ancient Israel, the cost involved was literally the expense of the animal being put to death. In modern times, the cost can come in the form of giving up money (by refusing the job promotion), or giving up something we really enjoy doing on Sunday morning (by serving at church), or giving up on purchasing something or forgoing a vacation so we can give to others (by supporting a ministry).

In this section of Romans, Paul describes what sacrificial *living* looks like for followers of Jesus. We surrender our whole lives to him, laying down our dreams, plans, and hopes for the one who gave his life for us. We make decisions every day to walk in the ways of Christ rather than following our own longings. We develop and deploy the spiritual gifts that God has given us. We love those who treat us as enemies and refuse to retaliate against them. As we live this way, we walk in the light of Jesus. *Sacrifice* is the lifestyle of every passionate follower of Jesus.

Giving God Everything [Romans 12:1-8]

[1] Therefore, I urge you, brothers and sisters, in view of God's mercy, to offer your bodies as a living sacrifice, holy and pleasing to God—this is your true and proper worship. [2] Do not conform to the pattern of this world, but be transformed by the renewing of your mind. Then you will be able to test and approve what God's will is—his good, pleasing and perfect will.

[3] For by the grace given me I say to every one of you: Do not think of yourself more highly than you ought, but rather think of yourself with sober judgment, in accordance with the faith God has distributed to each of you. [4] For just as each of us has one body with many members, and these members do not all have the same function, [5] so in Christ we, though many, form one body, and each member belongs to all the others. [6] We have different gifts, according to the grace given to each of us. If your gift is prophesying, then prophesy in accordance with your faith; [7] if it is serving, then serve; if it is teaching, then teach; [8] if it is to encourage, then give encouragement; if it is giving, then give generously; if it is to lead, do it diligently; if it is to show mercy, do it cheerfully.

Original Meaning

Up to this point, Paul has focused on the theological aspects of his gospel. But now he turns to practical and ethical implications. He begins with a call for believers to respond to God's mercies by presenting themselves as "living sacrifices." This act of surrender is our "true and proper worship" (verse 1), made possible by the renewing of our minds (see verse 2). We offer ourselves not ignorantly, like animals brought to slaughter, but intelligently and willingly. This is the worship that pleases God—a lifestyle we commit to leading each day.

We live out this transformed existence in *community*. It begins with us thinking of ourselves humbly (with "sober judgment") and in accordance with the measure of faith "God has distributed" to us (verse 3).

What is this measure that Paul has in mind? While some believe Paul is referring to the specific amount of faith God has distributed to each person, he more likely means that the Christian faith in general is the standard of measurement—a standard that is the same for all believers. If this interpretation is correct, Paul is asking us to look carefully to the gospel and its requirements as we assess ourselves.

The church, Paul continues, is like a human body. It has many parts, each with its own function, but all the parts form one body—and each part is needed for the body to function as it should (see verses 4–5). If we are "in Christ" (verse 5), we are in his body, inescapably joined to the other members of our Christian community. For this reason, we are to use our gifts—prophesying, serving, teaching, encouraging, and the like—not for personal gain but for the edification of the church (see verses 6–8). Our obedience to Christ is not an isolated endeavor but one that thrives in community and reflects God's design for his people.

❖ What are some ways Paul envisions believers in Christ sacrificing their lives for the glory of God (in both attitude and actions)?

_____

_____

_____

Past to Present

Consider what this passage meant to the original readers and how it applies to us today.

Conformed or Transformed

If you want to make a sculpture, you can use a mold or use a chisel. Using a mold involves creating a framework based on a model and then pouring casting material into it. The material is conformed to the mold around it and comes out looking just like the original model. The process for using a chisel is more involved. You start with a block of stone and then chip away until it is transformed into the desired shape.

In your life, you can either be conformed to the model of this world or transformed by the renewing of your mind. The world urges you to look to your own interests first, seek vengeance, and pursue what it deems is valuable. But God wants you to look to the interests of others first, offer forgiveness, and pursue what he says is valuable. You can either be pressed into the model of this world or allow Jesus to chip away and shape you into his image. Which will you choose?

❖ What are ways the world has tried to conform you to its pattern?

_____

_____

_____

_____

❖ What are some of the ways you believe God is shaping you to be more like Christ?

_____

_____

_____

_____

Use Those Gifts!
Paul describes a number of gifts in this section of Romans that God provides to his followers. God wants us to discover what those gifts are so we can use them. He wants us to employ them to serve his people—for other followers of Jesus need what we have to offer. When we exercise the gifts God has placed within us, whatever those happen to be, the church is stronger and the message of Jesus goes out into the world with greater power. Our contribution is that important!

❖ How does Paul's analogy of the different parts of the body help you understand why God wants you to use your spiritual gifts?

_____

_____

_____

❖ What spiritual gift do you believe God has given to you? How are you using that gift to serve him, the church, and the world?

_____

_____

_____

Love in Action [Romans 12:9-21]

⁹ Love must be sincere. Hate what is evil; cling to what is good. ¹⁰ Be devoted to one another in love. Honor one another above yourselves. ¹¹ Never be lacking in zeal, but keep your spiritual fervor, serving the Lord. ¹² Be joyful in hope, patient in affliction, faithful in prayer. ¹³ Share with the Lord's people who are in need. Practice hospitality.

¹⁴ Bless those who persecute you; bless and do not curse. ¹⁵ Rejoice with those who rejoice; mourn with those who mourn. ¹⁶ Live in harmony with one another. Do not be proud, but be willing to associate with people of low position. Do not be conceited.

¹⁷ Do not repay anyone evil for evil. Be careful to do what is right in the eyes of everyone. ¹⁸ If it is possible, as far as it depends on you, live at peace with everyone. ¹⁹ Do not take revenge, my dear friends, but leave room for God's wrath, for it is written: "It is mine to avenge; I will repay," says the Lord. ²⁰ On the contrary:

"If your enemy is hungry, feed him;
    if he is thirsty, give him something to drink.
In doing this, you will heap burning coals on his head."

²¹ Do not be overcome by evil, but overcome evil with good.

Original Meaning

Paul shifts tone in verse 9, moving to a rapid series of practical commands. His theme revolves around fostering a humble and peaceable attitude toward others, both within the church (see verses 10, 13, 16) and toward non-Christians (see verses 14, 17–21). At the heart of Paul's teaching is a call for *sincere* love, which he defines through specific behaviors that indicate a person is walking in step with the Holy Spirit. Paul's words are consistent with the teachings of Jesus, who likewise emphasized that love for God and others is central to the new covenant (see Mark 12:28–34; John 13:34–35).

Paul describes love as an active *choice* rather than a feeling. As believers in Christ, we are called to detest evil while clinging to good, exhibit devotion to our fellow believers, and honor others by putting their needs above our own desires (see Romans 12:9–10). Paul's commands regarding zeal and service in verse 11 likely allude to the Holy Spirit fueling our passion for God's work. Additionally, his statements in verses 12–13 emphasize steadfastness through hope, patience in trials, and dedication to prayer, equally paired with tangible acts of generosity and hospitality as evidence of love in action.

Paul expands his focus in verses 14–21 to include relationships with non-Christians. His commands here mirror Jesus' teachings in the Sermon on the Mount on practicing love in the midst of opposition (see Matthew 5:38–48). Paul exhorts believers to bless those who persecute them, advocating for a nonretaliatory ethic that prioritizes kindness and peace whenever possible (see Romans 12:17–18). By responding to enemies with love and care, we can reflect Christlike humility and potentially lead others to repentance (see verse 20). Paul underscores this overarching principle in verse 21, instructing each of us to overcome evil with good and ensure that our conduct remains aligned with God's will. This call to embody God's grace and exhibit sincere love demonstrates the heart of Christian discipleship.

❖ What are five actions of love in this passage that jump out at you?

_____

_____

_____

_____

Past to Present

Practicing Sincere Love

The Greek behind Paul's phrase "love must be sincere" (verse 9) contains no verb. A literal rendering would actually be "the love sincere." Supplying this imperative verb (as almost all translations do) is not necessarily wrong but obscures the fact that these words seem to be a heading for the rest of the passage. It is as if Paul is giving a definition of what *sincere* (literally nonhypocritical) love looks like. Christians can avoid love that is mere "playacting" if they choose to put into practice the commands that Paul will go on to describe.

Sincere love is a way for us to offer our "bodies as a living sacrifice" in a manner that is "holy and pleasing to God" (verse 1). It compels us to live in community and sacrificially offer ourselves so that others can benefit. This might take the form of extending hospitality, showing up at a hospital, cooking a meal, attending a friend's concert or sports event, or even giving blood when someone needs it. Whatever form it takes, sincere love is always authentic in that no self-interest is involved. We truly seek to actively honor others above ourselves.

❖ What does it mean for you to act in a *sincere* way in your relationships with others?

_____

_____

_____

_____

❖ How are you practicing the sacrificial love that Paul describes?

_____

_____

_____

_____

Returning Good for Evil

Paul was no stranger to persecution. In one letter, he describes receiving forty lashes, being beaten with rods and pelted with rocks, and generally living in danger from both Jews and Gentiles (see 2 Corinthians 11:24–26). Still, Paul could quote Jesus' teaching in advising his fellow believers to "bless those who curse you" (Luke 6:28).

As followers of Jesus, we are to seek to "do what is right in the eyes of everyone" and, as much as it is possible, "live at peace with everyone" (Romans 12:17–18). We are not to seek revenge but to trust God when he says, "It is mine to avenge; I will repay" (Deuteronomy 32:35). As we show kindness to our enemies—revealing we are being transformed in our minds and not conformed to the pattern of this world—we become witnesses of Jesus' love to those who need to experience it.

❖ What, if anything, tends to get in the way of you returning kindness to people who wrong you?

_____

_____

_____

_____

❖ Why is it often so hard *not* to seek vengeance against others?

_____

_____

_____

_____

Clothed in Christ [Romans 13:8-14]

⁸ Let no debt remain outstanding, except the continuing debt to love one another, for whoever loves others has fulfilled the law. ⁹ The commandments, "You shall not commit adultery," "You shall not murder," "You shall not steal," "You shall not covet," and whatever other command there may be, are summed up in this one command: "Love your neighbor as yourself." ¹⁰ Love does no harm to a neighbor. Therefore love is the fulfillment of the law.

¹¹ And do this, understanding the present time: The hour has already come for you to wake up from your slumber, because our salvation is nearer now than when we first believed. ¹² The night is nearly over; the day is almost here. So let us put aside the deeds of darkness and put on the armor of light. ¹³ Let us behave decently, as in the daytime, not in carousing and drunkenness, not in sexual immorality and debauchery, not in dissension and jealousy. ¹⁴ Rather, clothe yourselves with the Lord Jesus Christ, and do not think about how to gratify the desires of the flesh.

Original Meaning

Paul introduces the idea of "debt" in Romans 13:8 as a way of returning to his discussion on sincere love. The apostle, drawing on Leviticus 19:18 and Matthew 22:36–40, explains that sincere love for others upholds all the commandments of the law, for commands such as avoiding adultery, murder, theft, and covetousness naturally flow from the principle of loving one's neighbor. Paul's statement "love does no harm to a neighbor" (Romans 13:10) underscores that behaving like a Christian is not about rule-following but genuinely caring for others. This echoes Jesus' teaching to love as he loved (see Matthew 5:43–45).

Paul develops this thought by highlighting the urgency of living a life rooted in love and righteousness. He uses the imagery of waking from sleep and casting off the deeds of darkness because "our salvation is nearer now than when we first believed" (Romans 13:11). This eschatological perspective reminds us to understand the present time as a pivotal moment in the unfolding of God's plan. The approaching "day" refers to the return of Christ and the completion of God's redemptive work. We are to prepare for this day by living as children of light, displaying behavior that honors God and aligns with his purpose.

Paul concludes with an exhortation to "clothe [ourselves] with the Lord Jesus Christ" (verse 14). This metaphor signifies an intentional decision to model our lives after Christ's example. Instead of being driven by selfish desires, we are called to embody Jesus' nature—to "envelop" ourselves with him in such a way that he directs all our thinking and conduct. Such action requires the daily commitment of walking with Christ. In this way, we reflect his light to the world, fulfill our calling to love others, and live in readiness for our Savior's return.

❖ What debt are you as a follower of Jesus to leave outstanding? What are you to recognize about the "day" and "hour" in which you live?

_____

_____

_____

_____

Past to Present

Debt of Love

There is nothing quite like the feeling of paying off a debt. The joy you experience when you make a final student loan payment. The relief you feel when the credit balance is finally at zero. Even paying friends back for a restaurant bill they covered feels good. There is a sense of freedom and release when the burden of debt is finally out of your life.

However, there is one debt you should be glad you cannot repay. Paul says you are to have "the continuing debt to love one another" (verse 8), which implies other believers are to have a continuing debt of love toward you. This is how life should function in the body of Christ. You were never intended to get to the point where you feel your obligation to love others has been paid or their obligation to love you has been fulfilled. Rather, the goal is to remember the debt that Jesus paid on your behalf because he loved you—and then love others that way.

❖ Who is someone in your life you just find difficult to love? How could remembering the debt Jesus paid on your behalf help you to better love that person?

_____

_____

_____

_____

❖ Who are some of the people in your life who have gone out of their way to show love to you? What have you learned from those people about how to love others?

_____

_____

_____

_____

Clothed with Christ

Are you a person who loves fashion? You enjoy experimenting with different styles, colors, and patterns with your wardrobe. You watch for the latest trends from designers and look for ways to adapt them to your style. You look forward to taking shopping trips to your favorite stores so you can see all the latest offerings that are there—and maybe take them home. The clothes you wear can say a lot about who you are. In fact, if you are a "fashion enthusiast," you might even view your clothing as a way to communicate your personality and mood.

Consider this in light of Paul's command to "clothe yourselves with the Lord Jesus Christ" (verse 14). In the same way your physical clothes can represent to others who you are as a person, so your spiritual clothes can represent to others who you are in Christ. Are you wearing the same clothes as the world and conforming to its ideas of what looks good? Or are you wearing clothes that make you stand out for Christ and embody what he considers good? What you are "wearing" matters . . . especially when it comes to clothing yourself with Christ.

❖ What might the spiritual "clothes" you are wearing each day be communicating to others about your priorities and values?

_____

_____

_____

_____

❖ How would you describe what it means to clothe yourself with Christ? What are some of the traits of Jesus that you would especially like to put on—and why those traits?

_____

_____

_____

_____

Closing Prayer: Jesus, you have given yourself as a sacrifice for me—a debt I acknowledge I could never repay. I surrender my life to you day by day and moment by moment. Teach me to walk in your ways. Give me power to declare your will be done on this earth instead of my own. Spirit of God, open my eyes to your will and help me follow your Word. I pray today that my life will be a living sacrifice that brings honor to you, my God and Savior. Amen.

11

No Stumbling Blocks

Romans 14:1–12, 13–23; 15:1–13

A handbook given to British athletes in the 1924 Summer Olympics proclaimed, "To play the game is the only thing in life that matters." Eric Liddell, considered Britain's best hope of winning the 100 meters, felt otherwise. In the fall of 1923, he learned the heats for his best event were scheduled on a Sunday. Rather than compete on the Sabbath, he gave up his spot and trained for the 200-meter and 400-meter races. Surprisingly, as documented in *Chariots of Fire*, Liddell won bronze in the 200 meters. He won gold in the 400 meters, breaking the world record even though he had run it competitively only a handful of times.

Liddell's story illustrates a tension that exists between followers of Jesus. The fourth commandment that God gave to his people required them to "remember the Sabbath" and "not do any work" on it (Exodus 20:8, 10). But does that command apply to Christians? Or are we free from any such restrictions? What about other behaviors the Bible does not explicitly define as sin but are matters of conscience between believers? What should a faithful follower of Jesus do in those situations?

This is the issue Paul addresses in this next section of Romans. Interestingly, the position he takes is not so much about which *side* is correct but whether *all* believers are respecting, honoring, and loving one another. As he instructs, "Make up your mind not to put any stumbling block or obstacle in the way of a brother or sister" (14:13). Paul understood we *all* need support from our fellow believers to help us lead godly lives. For this reason, we *all* must be aware of behaviors that could cause our fellow brothers and sisters in Christ to stumble.

Do Not Judge [Romans 14:1–12]

[1] Accept the one whose faith is weak, without quarreling over disputable matters. [2] One person's faith allows them to eat anything, but another, whose faith is weak, eats only vegetables. [3] The one who eats everything must not treat with contempt the one who does not, and the one who does not eat everything must not judge the one who does, for God has accepted them. [4] Who are you to judge someone else's servant? To their own master, servants stand or fall. And they will stand, for the Lord is able to make them stand.

[5] One person considers one day more sacred than another; another considers every day alike. Each of them should be fully convinced in their own mind. [6] Whoever regards one day as special does so to the Lord. Whoever eats meat does so to the Lord, for they give thanks to God; and whoever abstains does so to the Lord and gives thanks to God. [7] For none of us lives for ourselves alone, and none of us dies for ourselves alone. [8] If we live, we live for the Lord; and if we die, we die for the Lord. So, whether we live or die, we belong to the Lord. [9] For this very reason, Christ died and returned to life so that he might be the Lord of both the dead and the living.

[10] You, then, why do you judge your brother or sister? Or why do you treat them with contempt? For we will all stand before God's judgment seat. [11] It is written:

"'As surely as I live,' says the Lord,
'every knee will bow before me;
    every tongue will acknowledge God.'"

[12] So then, each of us will give an account of ourselves to God.

Original Meaning

The church in Rome was divided into two groups: those "weak [in faith]" (14:1) and those "strong [in faith]" (15:1). Paul urges the strong believers to "accept the one whose faith is weak" and not allow differences over "disputable matters" (14:1) to interfere with their fellowship. As an example, he cites a dispute taking place over dietary practices. Paul insists neither group should condemn the other (see verse 3).

Paul also mentions disagreements in the church regarding sacred days (likely referring to Jewish holy observances). He asserts that whether they regard certain days as sacred or not, or whether they choose to eat or abstain from meat, they must all act out of sincere devotion to God (see verses 5–6). This mutual respect for differing practices is rooted in the fact that "none of us lives for ourselves alone, and none of us dies for ourselves alone" (verse 7), for in life and in death, we all belong to Christ. Our actions should always honor him.

Paul stresses judgment is God's alone. He confronts the believers' critical tendencies, asking, "Why do you judge your brother or sister?" (verse 10). He warns they will all one day stand before God's judgment seat, adding support from Isaiah 45:23 to reinforce God's sovereignty. Paul's teaching in this section serves as both a correction and a reassurance. It emphasizes that while differences in convictions exist among believers, they should not divide the body of Christ. This call to humility and grace will resonate throughout the chapter, underscoring Paul's vision of a unified church living in mutual love and harmony.

❖ How would you describe the disputes between the different groups in Rome? What marked their lifestyles and attitudes?

_____

_____

_____

_____

Past to Present

Consider what this passage meant to the original readers and how it applies to us today.

Disputable Matters

One believer attends a church where the worship music is performed by a band; another goes to a church with a choir. One Christian observes holy days on the calendar; another follows a more informal approach. These are examples of "disputable matters." They are gray areas in which the Bible does not spell out clear guidelines.

These kinds of matters should never divide a church. While tolerance should never be applied to situations the Bible clearly defines as sin—a vital point in this discussion—there are many times when disagreements between Christians just come down to preferences. The positions held by each side are both "acceptable" before God, and thus neither side should condemn the other for holding that particular position. As Paul wrote to another congregation, "I appeal to you . . . that you be perfectly united in mind and thought" (1 Corinthians 1:10).

❖ How should you treat those who don't see things exactly as you do?

_____

_____

_____

_____

❖ When is a time that you engaged with another believer in a disputable matter? What was the end result of your disagreement?

_____

_____

_____

_____

Perspective on Freedom

Paul does not mention observance of the Sabbath explicitly when he refers to believers considering "one day more sacred than another" (verse 5). However, the Sabbath was the most prominent of Jewish holy days, so we can assume it was part of the debate. We can picture the Jewish Christians arguing the Sabbath still needed to be observed, while the Gentile Christians argued such commands were no longer incumbent on believers. Overall, the attitude in the New Testament toward the Sabbath is that Christians are not required to treat it as a day of *rest*—though they are required to treat it as a day of *worship* to God.

This means it is not prohibited to take a job that requires working on Sunday, or washing your car on Sunday, or playing basketball on Sunday. You have the *liberty* to rest. Likewise, Sunday worship is not *mandated* in the New Testament (though it is a pattern). What matters are your priorities. Yes, you could do your regular work on Sunday, but does that demonstrate you are prioritizing your worship of God? The key is to develop a rhythm of gathering with fellow Christians to lift up your Creator and to make the space regularly to worship the Lord God.

❖ What are your views about having a Sabbath day of rest? What practices do you follow to refresh and strengthen your soul?

_____

_____

_____

_____

❖ How do you make praise and adoration of God a priority in your life (both on your own and in community)?

_____

_____

_____

_____

Choose Peace [Romans 14:13–23]

¹³ Therefore let us stop passing judgment on one another. Instead, make up your mind not to put any stumbling block or obstacle in the way of a brother or sister. ¹⁴ I am convinced, being fully persuaded in the Lord Jesus, that nothing is unclean in itself. But if anyone regards something as unclean, then for that person it is unclean. ¹⁵ If your brother or sister is distressed because of what you eat, you are no longer acting in love. Do not by your eating destroy someone for whom Christ died. ¹⁶ Therefore do not let what you know is good be spoken of as evil. ¹⁷ For the kingdom of God is not a matter of eating and drinking, but of righteousness, peace and joy in the Holy Spirit, ¹⁸ because anyone who serves Christ in this way is pleasing to God and receives human approval.

¹⁹ Let us therefore make every effort to do what leads to peace and to mutual edification. ²⁰ Do not destroy the work of God for the sake of food. All food is clean, but it is wrong for a person to eat anything that causes someone else to stumble. ²¹ It is better not to eat meat or drink wine or to do anything else that will cause your brother or sister to fall.

²² So whatever you believe about these things keep between yourself and God. Blessed is the one who does not condemn himself by what he approves. ²³ But whoever has doubts is condemned if they eat, because their eating is not from faith; and everything that does not come from faith is sin.

Original Meaning

Paul's command to "stop passing judgment on one another" (verse 13) sums up his thoughts on the importance of unity within the community. Both those who are "weak" and those who are "strong" are to accept one another as members of Christ's body. Critically, we are not to put a "stumbling block" or "obstacle" in the way of other believers. If we believe we are spiritually mature, we should do everything we can to avoid bringing spiritual downfall to another follower of Jesus. Maturity in the faith means prioritizing love over personal liberty.

Paul acknowledges all food is fundamentally clean (see verse 14) but urges sensitivity toward those for whom certain foods remain unclean due to their upbringing. Forcing such believers to act against their convictions could "destroy" them in their faith (verse 15). Furthermore, strong believers must avoid flaunting their freedom in ways that alienate or harm weaker Christians. Rather, *all* believers are to focus on righteousness, peace, and joy in the Holy Spirit (see verse 17). These reflect kingdom values that should guide all actions and relationships within the church, fostering mutual edification and harmony.

Ultimately, Paul calls both the strong and weak to live out these principles with humility. He reiterates the strong are to refrain from practices—such as eating certain foods or drinking wine—that might harm a fellow believer's conscience (see verse 21). Instead, they are to keep their personal convictions private and act in love (see verses 22–23). Paul's broader message here again underscores a critical principle for Christian living: placing communal well-being above personal freedoms and striving for unity within the body of Christ.

❖ What is Paul inviting Christians to do as an act of service and love? How do you think his readers responded to this challenge?

Past to Present

Strong Versus Weak

Paul frequently refers to strong versus weak believers in this chapter of Romans. In making this distinction, he is *not* saying the weak believers are those who have a susceptibility to a particular vice and the strong believers should abstain from a certain practice because that example may lead the weak into a life of degradation. The "weakness" Paul is addressing is spiritual—an inability for those believers to see that their faith allows them to do the behavior.

The point, once again, is for believers to show love for one another. A great way to do that is by not putting a stumbling block or obstacle in another believer's path! Paul's statement in verse 22 sums it up nicely: "Blessed is the one who does not condemn himself by what he approves." You can exercise your freedom in Christ and not be condemned before God. But if in exercising your freedom you are not demonstrating your love for other believers, you are not truly loving others.

❖ What is an example of behavior you once considered off-limits to Christians but now you see as a "disputable matter"?

_____

_____

_____

_____

❖ What is an example of how you have willingly limited your freedom for the sake of another believer?

_____

_____

_____

_____

Health of the Body

The US Declaration of Independence states that its citizens have the right to "life, liberty, and the pursuit of happiness." Other countries around the world have similar documents that articulate the rights of their particular citizens. Our culture also insists on specific rights for people—all of which is good and necessary for society to function. However, it is easy to take these concepts of individual rights and freedom into the church. It seems odd to willingly lay down those rights.

The truth is that the health of the body of Christ is more important than the rights of its individual members. Previously, Paul wrote that each member in the body of Christ "belongs to all the others" (12:5). This is why we are encouraged to exercise our spiritual gifts—for the edification of the overall body. Love for each other must remain at the forefront of our attitudes and actions. When we willingly lay down our rights for the sake of another, we demonstrate not only humility before God but also that we have sincere love for others.

❖ What is your attitude when it comes to willingly laying down your rights for another believer? What tends to make it hard for you to put aside those rights?

❖ When was a time you willingly limited your freedom for the sake of someone? How did God use that moment to bless that person and deepen your faith?

Bearing in Love [Romans 15:1–13]

[1] We who are strong ought to bear with the failings of the weak and not to please ourselves. [2] Each of us should please our neighbors for their

good, to build them up. [3] For even Christ did not please himself but, as it is written: "The insults of those who insult you have fallen on me." [4] For everything that was written in the past was written to teach us, so that through the endurance taught in the Scriptures and the encouragement they provide we might have hope.

[5] May the God who gives endurance and encouragement give you the same attitude of mind toward each other that Christ Jesus had, [6] so that with one mind and one voice you may glorify the God and Father of our Lord Jesus Christ.

[7] Accept one another, then, just as Christ accepted you, in order to bring praise to God. [8] For I tell you that Christ has become a servant of the Jews on behalf of God's truth, so that the promises made to the patriarchs might be confirmed [9] and, moreover, that the Gentiles might glorify God for his mercy. As it is written:

"Therefore I will praise you among the Gentiles;
   I will sing the praises of your name."

[10] Again, it says,

"Rejoice, you Gentiles, with his people."

[11] And again,

"Praise the Lord, all you Gentiles;
   let all the peoples extol him."

[12] And again, Isaiah says,

"The Root of Jesse will spring up,
   one who will arise to rule over the nations;
   in him the Gentiles will hope."

[13] May the God of hope fill you with all joy and peace as you trust in him, so that you may overflow with hope by the power of the Holy Spirit.

Original Meaning

Paul urges the "strong" (with whom he now identifies) and the "weak" to prioritize unity and love within their community. He encourages those who understand that their faith allows them more freedom to bear with the limitations of the weak who cannot yet accept such freedoms. This not a call for believers to merely tolerate differences but to actively support one another (see verses 1–2). Paul points to Jesus as the ultimate example, quoting Psalm 69:9 to highlight how he endured insults for God's glory (see verse 3). Paul reminds the Roman church that Scripture is rich with lessons intended to teach, inspire hope, and offer encouragement and endurance for all who seek unity in faith.

This unity, according to Paul, is not rooted in conformity of thought but in a shared purpose and an alignment "that Christ Jesus had" (verse 5). Paul prays for the community to possess a spirit of unity that transcends differences in opinions while reflecting the love and character of Christ. The ultimate purpose of this unity is to glorify God with one voice and heart as a diverse yet harmonized body of believers (see verse 6). This prayer serves as a reminder that the church's central goal is mutual edification and collective worship, which requires setting aside personal preferences for the greater good of God's community.

Paul concludes with a command to "accept one another . . . as Christ accepted you" (verse 7). We are not to just *tolerate* but *welcome* one another as brothers and sisters in the body of Christ—and we do so because Jesus has welcomed us. Paul draws on the three sections of Jewish Scriptures (Torah, Prophets, and Writings) in verses 9–12 to show how Jesus became "a servant of the Jews on behalf of God's truth" to confirm his promises to the patriarchs and so "the Gentiles might glorify God for his mercy" (verses 8–9). What unites believers is a shared hope in Christ, the root of Jesse, who brings salvation to all. Only when Jew and Gentile rejoice together in their common hope will they be able to praise God as he wants to be praised.

❖ What does Paul urge the strong in faith to do as it relates to the weak in faith? What traits of Jesus does he ask all believers to model?

_____

_____

_____

_____

Past to Present

Modeled After Christ

When you are learning something new, it is helpful to have an example to follow. A picture of a completed desk can help you know how to build a desk. A video of a person showing you how he planted his garden can help you know how to plant your garden. A runner who shares the routine she follows to train for a marathon can help you prepare to run a marathon. The same is true when it comes to the family of God.

Paul points out in this part of Romans that Jesus "did not please himself" but willingly endured the "insults" and scorn that people were directing at God (verse 3). Jesus, as powerful as he was, willingly gave up his right to life itself for the sake of others. If Christ can do this, then certainly the "strong" members of his family can give up their rights to do the things that cause distress in the "weak" members of his family. We should all be willing to follow Jesus' example in giving up our personal freedoms for the greater good of showing God's love.

❖ Who has served as a good role model of the Christian faith in your life? What did that person do that helped you understand what it means to live as a Christian?

_____

_____

_____

_____

❖ How are you modeling the example of Jesus when it comes to bearing with others in love? What could you do this week to better model Jesus' example?

_____

_____

_____

_____

Balance Is Critical

Balance is critical in life. Working at your job is important in providing for your family, but if all you do is work, your family will wonder why they never see you. Relaxing with your family is important, but if that is all you do, your family will wonder why you aren't earning money working at a job. Balance is critical as well in understanding the message of Romans. On the one hand, Paul makes it clear that God, through Jesus, is transforming *individuals*. Yet, on the other hand, it is also clear that God, through Jesus, is forming a *community*.

The heart of the gospel is the message of God's justifying work in Christ. Our preaching and teaching must therefore confront *individuals* with sin and offer them redemption in Christ. But God also wants to create *communities* of people who have been transformed by the gospel. Faithfulness to the gospel demands that we maintain a balance between the two perspectives. The gospel does more than just rescue us from hell. It also radically transforms us, bringing us into reconciliation with other followers of Jesus as well as with God.

❖ What are some of the ways the gospel has transformed your life as an *individual*?

_____

_____

_____

_____

❖ What are some of the ways the gospel has brought you into *community* with others?

_____

_____

_____

_____

_____

_____

Closing Prayer: *Heavenly Father, help me to put love of others above any selfish desires that I have in pursuing my own rights, freedoms, and ways. I pray that your Holy Spirit would search my heart and change my life. I don't want to ever be a stumbling block for others. Rather, I want to model the example your Son set when he was on this earth. Give me power to extend your love in every relationship in my life. For your glory, I pray. Amen.*

12

Stories of Friendship

Romans 15:14–33; 16:1–16, 17–27

Perhaps you have heard the phrase "flyover country." The term refers to the interior regions of the United States that lie between the more populated East and West Coasts. Many people see these parts of the country only when they "fly over" them by air. They never actually see them in person at ground level . . . and thus miss out on seeing some amazing places. After all, flyover country includes astounding sites such as the Grand Canyon, Yellowstone National Park, the Rockies, Mount Rushmore, and the "fruited plains" of Middle America.

When it comes to the last chapters in Romans, you might be tempted to treat them as "flyover country." Some of the content reads like a sign-off from Paul with a blessing for the church. Some of it feels like a travel itinerary, with the apostle relating his plans to stop by and visit the community on his way to Spain. Much of it—actually, all of the last chapter—is a list of names of people whom Paul is commending to the church or to whom he is passing along his greetings. After such a deeply theological book, the ending seems a bit anticlimactic, and we might be tempted to skim past the words or skip these chapters altogether.

So here is the invitation. Slow down as you come to the end of this rich and personal letter and consider what Paul has written. Each name recorded carries a story of friendship, partnership in the gospel, and life shared. Each greeting is extended to a brother or sister in the faith whom you will meet in heaven one day. Every stroke of the pen is still inspired by the Spirit of the living God. Don't miss the richness of these final words. Refuse to fly over this part of Romans. Slow down, dig in, and let the Spirit of God minister to your soul.

Ministry to the World [Romans 15:14–33]

[14] I myself am convinced, my brothers and sisters, that you yourselves are full of goodness, filled with knowledge and competent to instruct one another. [15] Yet I have written you quite boldly on some points to remind you of them again, because of the grace God gave me [16] to be a minister of Christ Jesus to the Gentiles. He gave me the priestly duty of proclaiming the gospel of God, so that the Gentiles might become an offering acceptable to God, sanctified by the Holy Spirit.

[17] Therefore I glory in Christ Jesus in my service to God. [18] I will not venture to speak of anything except what Christ has accomplished through me in leading the Gentiles to obey God by what I have said and done— [19] by the power of signs and wonders, through the power of the Spirit of God. So from Jerusalem all the way around to Illyricum, I have fully proclaimed the gospel of Christ. [20] It has always been my ambition to preach the gospel where Christ was not known, so that I would not be building on someone else's foundation. [21] Rather, as it is written:

"Those who were not told about him will see,
and those who have not heard will understand."

[22] This is why I have often been hindered from coming to you.

[23] But now that there is no more place for me to work in these regions, and since I have been longing for many years to visit you, [24] I plan to do so when I go to Spain. I hope to see you while passing through and to have you assist me on my journey there, after I have enjoyed your company for a while. [25] Now, however, I am on my way to Jerusalem in the service of the Lord's people there. [26] For Macedonia and Achaia were

pleased to make a contribution for the poor among the Lord's people in Jerusalem. [27] They were pleased to do it, and indeed they owe it to them. For if the Gentiles have shared in the Jews' spiritual blessings, they owe it to the Jews to share with them their material blessings. [28] So after I have completed this task and have made sure that they have received this contribution, I will go to Spain and visit you on the way. [29] I know that when I come to you, I will come in the full measure of the blessing of Christ.

[30] I urge you, brothers and sisters, by our Lord Jesus Christ and by the love of the Spirit, to join me in my struggle by praying to God for me. [31] Pray that I may be kept safe from the unbelievers in Judea and that the contribution I take to Jerusalem may be favorably received by the Lord's people there, [32] so that I may come to you with joy, by God's will, and in your company be refreshed. [33] The God of peace be with you all. Amen.

Original Meaning

Paul's prayer-wish in Romans 15:13 marks the end of the body of the letter. What remains is the closing. Paul begins by explaining why he has written to them so "boldly" (verse 15), stating his intent was to remind them of the gospel truths they already understood. He commends them for their goodness and knowledge, showing both diplomacy and humility as he articulates his mission of bringing the Gentiles to God (see verse 16). The priestly language Paul uses reinforces his view of his ministry as a divine vocation. He takes "glory in Christ" (verse 17) for enabling him to preach the gospel from Jerusalem to Illyricum.

Paul states that his focus remains preaching the gospel wherever Christ is not yet known (see verse 20). For this reason, he intends to take the gospel to Spain—but will visit the congregation in Rome on his way there (see verses 23–24). However, before he does this, he first must travel to Jerusalem to deliver a monetary collection gathered from the Gentile churches for the impoverished Jewish Christians (see verses 25–26). These Gentile churches "were pleased to do it" (verse 27), for they recognize the spiritual debt they owe to the Jewish people. Paul's hope is for the offering to serve as a bridge between the two groups, fostering reconciliation and demonstrating the tangible love of the broader Christian community.

Paul concludes with a heartfelt request for the believers' prayers. He asks them to intercede for his safety from unbelievers in Judea and for the church in Jerusalem to accept the collection (see verses 30–31). He reiterates that his desire is to come to the Romans (verse 32). His prayer for peace (see verse 33) encapsulates his longing for unity within the diverse Christian community and reflects his trust in God to fulfill his purposes. Paul makes it evident that he is dedicated to his apostolic mission and pastoral care for the church. He relies on Jesus for both the success of his ministry and the spiritual growth of the believers.

❖ What are some of the reasons Paul gives for writing "boldly" to the Roman Christians? What does he reiterate to them about his primary ambition and mission?

_____

_____

_____

_____

_____

Past to Present

Consider what this passage meant to the original readers and how it applies to us today.

Open and Closed Doors

Perhaps you've heard the expression, "God opens some doors and closes others." The idea behind the idiom is that God sovereignly directs the course of all your steps. Sometimes, he closes a door by shutting off an opportunity that you were pursuing. Other times, he opens a door by providing a new opportunity that you might not have considered. God does this to lead you into those places in life where he wants you to go.

Paul understood this idea of open and closed doors. He considered his ministry of sharing the gospel in the East to be fulfilled—a door that God had closed. But now he saw new opportunities to share the gospel in the West—a door that God was opening—and hoped the Roman Christians would assist him in the endeavor. Importantly, Paul never allowed a closed door to derail his mission. Instead, he looked for the new doors that God was opening. The same should be true in the life and ministry of every follower of Christ.

❖ When has God used an open door to lead you into a new opportunity? How did you recognize that he was opening that door?

_____

_____

_____

_____

❖ When has God used a closed door to shut off an opportunity? How did you respond when you realized that door was closing?

_____

_____

_____

_____

Struggling in Prayer

Paul invites the Roman Christians to join in his "struggle" by praying for him (verse 30). Specifically, he asks them to pray that he will "be kept safe from the unbelievers in Judea" and that the financial offering from the Gentile churches will "be favorably received by the Lord's people" in Jerusalem (verse 31). Regarding the first point, unbelieving Jews were especially hostile to Paul for opening the doors of God's goodness to the Gentiles. Regarding the second, the Jewish Christians could refuse the gift as being tainted by the "unclean hands" of Gentiles. Paul saw both of these as spiritual issues that needed to be contended with in prayer.

There are times when prayer comes easy. But there are other times when prayer will be hard—when we need to struggle and contend in prayer against the spiritual forces in this world that are opposed to God and his will. We should be prepared to cry out to God at such times and endure even when we feel the weight of the warfare. There *will* be times when we must pray through the obstacles . . . and we should enter these struggles in prayer with other faithful believers.

❖ When is a time that you can remember struggling in prayer? What was the situation—and what was the outcome of your prayers?

_____

_____

_____

_____

_____

❖ Who are the people in your life who can enter the battle with you? How do you invite them consistently to enter into prayer with you?

_____

_____

_____

_____

_____

Heartfelt Greetings [Romans 16:1–16]

[1] I commend to you our sister Phoebe, a deacon of the church in Cenchreae. [2] I ask you to receive her in the Lord in a way worthy of his people and to give her any help she may need from you, for she has been the benefactor of many people, including me.

[3] Greet Priscilla and Aquila, my co-workers in Christ Jesus. [4] They risked their lives for me. Not only I but all the churches of the Gentiles are grateful to them.

[5] Greet also the church that meets at their house.

Greet my dear friend Epenetus, who was the first convert to Christ in the province of Asia.

[6] Greet Mary, who worked very hard for you.

[7] Greet Andronicus and Junia, my fellow Jews who have been in prison with me. They are outstanding among the apostles, and they were in Christ before I was.

[8] Greet Ampliatus, my dear friend in the Lord.

[9] Greet Urbanus, our co-worker in Christ, and my dear friend Stachys.

[10] Greet Apelles, whose fidelity to Christ has stood the test.

Greet those who belong to the household of Aristobulus.

[11] Greet Herodion, my fellow Jew.

Greet those in the household of Narcissus who are in the Lord.

[12] Greet Tryphena and Tryphosa, those women who work hard in the Lord.

Greet my dear friend Persis, another woman who has worked very hard in the Lord.

[13] Greet Rufus, chosen in the Lord, and his mother, who has been a mother to me, too.

[14] Greet Asyncritus, Phlegon, Hermes, Patrobas, Hermas and the other brothers and sisters with them.

[15] Greet Philologus, Julia, Nereus and his sister, and Olympas and all the Lord's people who are with them.

¹⁶ Greet one another with a holy kiss.

All the churches of Christ send greetings.

Original Meaning

Letters of commendation were important in the ancient world. People who traveled in an age with few public facilities depended on the help of people they had sometimes never met. Phoebe is evidently going to be traveling to Rome, so Paul commends to the church this "sister" and servant "of the church in Cenchreae" (verse 1). This woman, a "deacon," served the church by ministering to the financial and material needs of the believers. She used her wealth to support the church and its missionaries (like Paul). Her ministry made her worthy of a Christian greeting and any assistance the Roman church could give her.

The length of the greetings in verses 3–15 is unusual for Paul's letters. He greets twenty-seven individuals, two families, and three house churches by name. Notable among them are Priscilla and Aquila (see verse 3). This couple came to Corinth after fleeing Rome due to Claudius's expulsion order, ministered with Paul in Corinth, and engaged with him in ministry in Ephesus (see Acts 18:2–3, 18). They apparently served in Ephesus for some time before returning to Rome. They must have been fairly wealthy, for they owned a house large enough for a group of believers to meet there (see Romans 16:5).

Most of the names likely appear only here in Scripture. Epenetus is unique in that he was "the first convert to Christ in the province of Asia" (verse 5). Andronicus and Junia, probably husband and wife, were relatives of Paul and were in prison with him (likely for the sake of the gospel). Paul calls them "apostles," which in this context probably means commissioned missionaries (verse 7). The extensive mention of names serves to affirm Paul's personal connections and strengthen his bond with the church. Public recognition of these believers, as the letter was read aloud, fostered goodwill and unity within the community.

Paul concludes with an instruction to "greet one another with a holy kiss" (verse 16), a practice that symbolized peace and fellowship. Notably, Paul emphasizes these greetings come not only from him but also from all the churches of Christ, which highlights the broader community of faith. This concluding sentiment serves as a reminder of the interconnectedness of the global church, united in Christ, regardless of geography or individual differences.

❖ What insights do you gain about the members of the church in Rome as you read Paul's greetings and commendations?

_____

_____

_____

_____

_____

Past to Present

Acknowledging Service

Ten of the people Paul greets or commends in this section are women. He commends Phoebe for meeting the financial needs of God's people (see verse 2). He mentions Priscilla as his coworker in Christ (see verse 3). Junia is described as "outstanding among the apostles" (verse 7). Tryphena, Tryphosa, and Persis are commended for their work "in the Lord" (verse 12). Paul notes Mary "worked very hard" for the church (verse 6) and Rufus's mother was like a mother to him (see verse 13).

What is interesting is that Paul affirms the service of these women right alongside the men. In the first century, women were generally viewed as having a subordinate role in society and given limited rights and opportunities as compared to men. However, here we find Paul acknowledging the service of *both* men and women. In our lives—whether due to attitudes in society or our own doubts—we may wonder if God sees our acts of service. But the Bible is clear the Lord sees our good works and rewards us for them (see Matthew 6:2–4).

❖ When are a few times where you questioned whether your service to the Lord was being recognized by others or had any impact at all?

_____

_____

_____

_____

_____

❖ How does it encourage you to know that God sees your acts of service—even when nobody else does—and will reward you for it?

_____

_____

_____

_____

_____

Giving Honor

Many schools have an honor roll. This is a list of students who stand out for achieving a specific academic standard or meeting some other criteria of excellence the school sets. This is similar to what we find at the end of Romans. Paul is giving his "honor roll" of individuals in the Roman church who stand out in some way or another for their work and service to God. What is interesting is that Paul offers this honor regardless of the person's economic or social status.

What little evidence we have suggests that most of the early Christians came from the lower classes (see 1 Corinthians 1:26). This is not to say other classes were not represented (Priscilla and Aquila seem to have been relatively wealthy). But the reason Paul honored these men and women in the church was not because of their *status* but because of their *service*. This tells us that we should never question whether God can employ us in his kingdom work. He offers the opportunity—and honor—to all who serve him regardless of their position in society.

❖ Has there been a time when you questioned whether you could participate in God's work because of your status or something you did in the past that you felt "disqualified" you? If so, how did God reveal that he still wanted you to participate in his plans?

_____

_____

_____

_____

_____

❖ Who are some of the overlooked people in your life who are doing amazing things for God? What can you do this week to express your appreciation to them?

_____

_____

_____

_____

_____

Closing Warning and Blessing [Romans 16:17–27]

¹⁷ I urge you, brothers and sisters, to watch out for those who cause divisions and put obstacles in your way that are contrary to the teaching you have learned. Keep away from them. ¹⁸ For such people are not serving

our Lord Christ, but their own appetites. By smooth talk and flattery they deceive the minds of naive people. [19] Everyone has heard about your obedience, so I rejoice because of you; but I want you to be wise about what is good, and innocent about what is evil.

[20] The God of peace will soon crush Satan under your feet.

The grace of our Lord Jesus be with you.

[21] Timothy, my co-worker, sends his greetings to you, as do Lucius, Jason and Sosipater, my fellow Jews.

[22] I, Tertius, who wrote down this letter, greet you in the Lord.

[23] Gaius, whose hospitality I and the whole church here enjoy, sends you his greetings.

Erastus, who is the city's director of public works, and our brother Quartus send you their greetings. [24]

[25] Now to him who is able to establish you in accordance with my gospel, the message I proclaim about Jesus Christ, in keeping with the revelation of the mystery hidden for long ages past, [26] but now revealed and made known through the prophetic writings by the command of the eternal God, so that all the Gentiles might come to the obedience that comes from faith— [27] to the only wise God be glory forever through Jesus Christ! Amen.

Original Meaning

Paul touches on several different topics as he brings his letter to a close. One notable inclusion is his admonition against false teachers (see verses 17–19). Paul warns the believers to be vigilant against those who cause division and try to place obstacles in their faith. These individuals teach doctrines contrary to the gospel, serve their own desires, and cause harm by preying on the naive with persuasive words. Paul wants the Roman Christians to continue being "wise about what is good, and innocent about what is evil," remembering that "the God of peace will soon crush Satan under your feet" (verses 19–20).

Paul also includes greetings on behalf of his associates and fellow laborers in Christ. Timothy, who was among the most trusted of Paul's companions, is mentioned alongside others like Lucius, Jason, and Sosipater, all of whom served with Paul faithfully. Paul also acknowledges a man named Tertius, who was the scribe who transcribed the letter. Greetings from these individuals, as well as Gaius, Erastus, and Quartus, emphasize the close-knit community of believers working to spread the gospel. This section provides insight into the network of early Christians and demonstrates the mutual encouragement and hospitality evident among Paul's circle of collaborators.

The apostle finishes the letter with a doxology in which he praises God for the gospel revealed through Jesus (see verses 25–27). This proclamation highlights the mystery of God's redemptive plan, which is now made known to all nations. Paul underscores this revelation was foreseen in prophetic writings and brought to fulfillment by God's command so all people might respond with the obedience that springs from faith. Paul's doxology affirms the central message of Romans, pointing believers to worship and trust in the wisdom and power of God.

❖ How does Paul describe the actions of false teachers? Why do you think he wants the Roman Christians to watch out for them?

Past to Present

Beware of False Teachers

Today, teachers at a high school would rightly be called out by the administration if they were teaching a course in history, science, math, or any other subject that distorted the facts and represented their version of the topic. At the end of Romans, we find Paul doing much the same. While various theories exist about who exactly the false teachers were in Rome, we find Paul calling them out because they "cause divisions," "put obstacles" in the way of people's faith, and serve not "our Lord Christ, but their own appetites" (verses 17–18).

False teachers, both then and now, use "smooth talk and flattery" to "deceive the minds of naive people" (verse 18). This is why we, like the Roman Christians, must follow Paul's advice to "keep away from them" (verse 17) and be "wise about what is good" (verse 19). Jesus said, "If you hold to my teaching, you are really my disciples. Then you will know the truth, and the truth will set you free" (John 8:31–32). When we hold fast to Jesus' teaching, we know the truth of the gospel and are able to see through the deceptions of false teachers.

❖ What kind of destruction does Paul say false teachers sow in the church? What are some methods false teachers employ to get people to buy into their message?

_____

_____

_____

_____

_____

❖ What are some of the common false teachings that are present in the church today? How can believers identify and stand against these wolves in sheep's clothing?

_____

_____

_____

_____

_____

Praise God . . . Always!

Paul understood that he had received a "priestly duty of proclaiming the gospel of God" (Romans 15:16). He was God's "chosen instrument" to proclaim the message of salvation "to the Gentiles and their kings and to the people of Israel" (Acts 9:15). However, he also understood that only *God* could establish those who heard his message in the faith. The good news of redemption in Christ is the pinnacle of God's plan for humanity. It was the "mystery hidden for long ages past" but "now revealed and made known" (Romans 16:25–26).

Paul's response to this incredible work of "the only wise God" is to give him praise and "glory forever through Jesus Christ" (verse 27). This should be our response as well! When the truth is taught, we give glory to God. When the seed of the gospel is planted in a person's heart, we give praise to the Father. When a believer overcomes through the power of the Holy Spirit, we give thanks for that good work. All theology, such as we find in Romans, finds its ultimate goal in the *glory of God*. It enables us as God's people to glorify him more effectively and more passionately because we have learned more about him.

❖ What does Paul's doxology say to you about the gospel and the God you worship?

_____

_____

_____

❖ As you close this study, what declaration of praise do you want to make to God in regard to the truths you have learned about him?

_____

_____

_____

Closing Prayer: *Lord of life, I praise you for your sovereign rule and reign over all things. Thank you for revealing the "mystery" of your plan of salvation in Christ and for adopting me as your dearly beloved child. Help me today to be a dedicated messenger of the good news that I have received so the world may come to know about Jesus and be rescued from their sins. I give you all glory, honor, and praise for the work you have done in my life. In Jesus' name, I pray. Amen.*

About

KEVIN HARNEY and DOUGLAS J. MOO

Dr. Kevin G. Harney is the president and cofounder of Organic Outreach International and the teaching pastor of Shoreline Church in Monterey, California. He is the author of the *Organic Outreach* trilogy, *Organic Disciples*, more than one hundred small group guides, and numerous articles. He does extensive teaching and speaking nationally and internationally to equip leaders in effective and culture-changing discipleship and evangelism. He and his wife, Sherry, have three married sons, three daughters-in-law, and five grandchildren.

Douglas J. Moo (PhD, University of St. Andrews) is Emeritus Professor of Biblical Studies at Wheaton College and Distinguished Visiting Professor of New Testament at Phoenix Seminary. His work centers on understanding the text of the New Testament and its application today. He has written extensively in several commentary series, including the NIV Application Commentary and the New International Commentary on the New Testament. With his son Jonathan Moo, he coauthored *Creation Care: A Biblical Theology of the Natural World*, part of Zondervan's Biblical Theology for Life series.

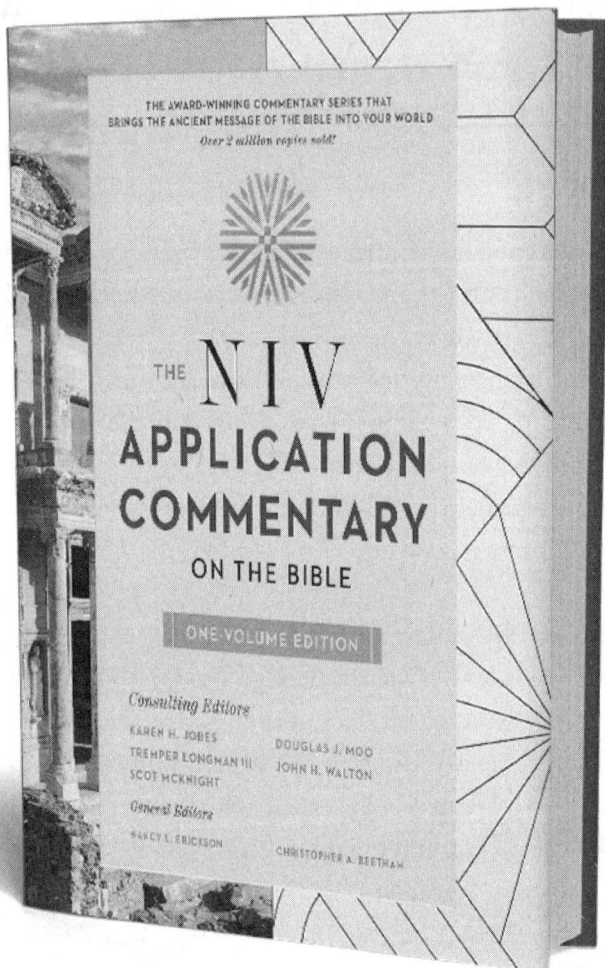